inside the **Jewelry Box**

A Collector's Guide to

Costume Jewelry

Identification and Values

Ann Mitchell Pitman

COLLECTOR BOOKS

A Division of Schroeder Publishing Co., Inc.

Cover design by Beth Summers
Book design by Kelly Dowdy

COLLECTOR BOOKS
P.O. Box 3009
Paducah, Kentucky 42002-3009
www.collectorbooks.com

Searching For A Publisher?

We are always looking for people knowledgeable within their fields. If you
feel that there is a real need for a book on your collectible subject and have a
large comprehensive collection, contact Collector Books.

Contents

Acknowledgments

When you sit down to thank all of the people who helped you make a wish come true, you realize how much help you really had, and how many people were there to lend those helping hands.

My daughter Ariel, your constant help and enthusiasm was invaluable, your research skills unequaled, and your patience admirable. For all the times I had to say, "No, I can't go right now," or "No, I can't do it right now," I appreciate your quiet acceptance. Although I am as proud of this book as I can possibly be, I am even more proud of the beautiful, intelligent, and amazing person you have become.

My dear friend Kim Paff was there from the very beginning and her touch is seen from the first page to the last. Kim shared her collection and took me to meet an extraordinary lady who shared her collection, and her recollections. A more kind and generous, giving and spiritual person you will never meet.

My little ditty grandmother, Frances Mildred "Midge" Gray Taylor Peden, who was glamorous even in sweatpants and sweatshirts, and whose one standard of beauty was bright red fingernail polish, I miss you every day. My great grandmother, Frances Berta Fennel Gray, who never left the house without gloves, and whose pocketbook and shoes always matched, thank you for my first exposure to glamour. I miss you too.

My mom and dad, Charlie and Jean Mitchell; I would need a separate book to tell you how much you both mean to me, and what I have learned from you. I hope that you are proud of me. Thanks for the tools, Dad, and thanks for the green thumb, Mom.
.

To fellow collectors Nancy Canãs, Georgia Robinson, Laurel Ladd Ciotti, and Patti Collins Bultman, thank you for opening your homes and your jewelry boxes. Oh, and thank you for letting me play with your jewelry.

To Carol Bell and Susan Klein of Treasures-in-Time at the Antique Center of Texas in Houston, thank you for sharing your treasures.

To Isabelle "Liz" Bryman and the members of Jewelcollect, who are always willing to share information and jewelry photos, I thank you. A list of contributors appears near the end of this book.

To Alice Leonard, who found my column and I our first "gig," God used you in a special way, and I am humbly grateful.

To Pat Seal, who always knows the answer, or knows where to find it, I thank you for always being there, via phone or computer, and for appreciating the urgency of a deadline. And for checking to make sure I was still alive in the midst of it. Thank you to Glendon Seal, who always has a kind word, who can make beautiful jewelry from scraps, and who always remembers to say "Hello!"

To Harrice Simons Miller, who years ago signed my dog-eared, tattered copy of her Second Edition, and treated me as an equal from the very beginning.

To authors Karima Parry, Cherri Simonds, and Ginger Moro, your books are invaluable to me, and to all collectors of Bakelite and vintage jewelry. I now can appreciate the true labors of love that your books represent.

To Bobye Syverson, thank you for your expertise on Eisenberg and for verifying genuine pieces. We anxiously await your book.

Van Dell floral spray brooch.

To Jill Gallina, who convinced me to make that crucial telephone call to Collector Books. You were confident it would want to publish my book; apparently, you were right.

To Gail Ashburn and Amy Sullivan at Collector Books, I can never thank you enough.

To John Rump and Park Place Jaguar in Houston, Texas, thanks for loaning me the black beauty. I look mah-velous! And to Adam Martinez, thank you for moving the Jaguar into the shade AND leaving the air conditioner running.

To Chad Garuette and Frank Wang at DPI Photo in Houston, Texas, thanks for the extra work and the special touch with the film processing.

Chandelier earring.

To my sister Sheen Mitchell Rogers, thanks for not stealing my Disneyland bracelet, like I stole your Sunday school pin. To my sister Glynnis Judy, thanks for always being excited about whatever jewelry I was wearing. And for keeping our great grandmother's mink poodle pin safe in your jewelry box. To my brother Charlie Mitchell, for making his dream come true. I love you all dearly.

To Blanche Gladis Poremba, thank you for always being ready for a telephone chat and for always being on my side, you always make me think I am special.

To Laurie Mills and Donna Burns, friends for fifteen years, you have always encouraged me and made me believe I could accomplish anything. Thank you for your love and your prayers.

In memoriam, to Carl "Pop" and Miss Molly Fowler, married 75 years before going home: You embraced me as a daughter and loved me unconditionally; my life has an empty spot where you used to be.

To Tony, who truly is my better half, I dedicate this book to you. I could not have done this without you, your love, your support, and your enthusiasm. You asked all the right questions, and reminded me that, after all, it WAS fun. You have been there for over 25 years, never complaining when it seemed like all I could talk about was jewelry. Thank you for "forcing" me to collect Bakelite by buying that first piece for me. Thank you for taking a photo of me that only someone who loves me could have done, with acceptance and great patience. You knew I could write a book even when I didn't know that I could. Your name belongs on the cover of this book as much as mine does, for all that you put up with all this time. I hope I am worth the trouble. Looks like we made it.

Floral parure.

About the Author

First bracelet ever purchased, Cinderella's Castle at Disneyland.

1969 was a year of firsts for me — first airplane ride, first time throwing up on an airplane, first time to California, first time to Disneyland . . . Before entering Disneyland, my parents gave my sisters, Sheen and Glynnis, and me, money for souvenirs. My brother Charlie was still in a stroller and didn't need any money. My one and only purchase was a silver-tone bracelet with a photo of Cinderella's castle on it. That bracelet was my first costume jewelry purchase.

My collecting began in earnest over twenty years later. I loved going to antique shops, malls, and shows. A local annual antiques show started the trip that ended with this book. Nestled among the free fliers and brochures on the table at the entrance was an antiques publication called *Antique-Week*. Inside was an ad saying it was looking for writers in South Carolina to cover shows and auctions. I had noticed an ad that morning in the local newspaper about a show and sale of antique jewelry and vintage posters. After attending, doing two interviews, and taking a few photos, I went home and wrote about the experience. A few weeks later my first byline appeared.

Throughout my writing and collecting career, luck and the grace of God have played heavy hands in my being at the right place at the right time, meeting the right people.

Close up of bracelet, fastened.

In 1996 my husband, Tony, got a computer; I sneaked in and played with it when he wasn't working. One night I stumbled across lizjewel.com and discovered Jewelcollect, an online email listserv of hundreds of costume jewelry collecting members. One of those members, Alice Leonard, told me I should be writing a column about costume jewelry, then proposed it to a friend of hers who just happened to own an antiques publication. *Inside the Jewelry Box* was launched.

Over the years, I have interviewed many members of Jewelcollect, who all willingly shared information and photos about either their favorite designer or collection. Many, such as Karima Parry, Cherri Simonds, Jill Gallina and Harrice Simons Miller, have written books about costume jewelry. I do not place myself in their category. These women are experts in their field; I am just a curious collector, gathering information and taking photographs, once again in the right place at the right time.

Oriental-style letter A rhinestone pin.

Unlike a collection such as pottery that sits on a shelf and is admired, costume jewelry is taken out and played with and lovingly worn. I encourage you to get out and meet other collectors of vintage costume jewelry. I met my very dear friend Kim Paff through Jewelcollect, and we have taken many trips together to meet other JCers and collectors. We have fun every single minute, and that is what a collection should be all about, don't you think?

Foreword

Welcome to the wonderful world of vintage costume jewelry collecting. Throughout the antiques world there are a great many categories of things most collectible: furniture; glass, china, and porcelain; dolls and toys, even (with a nod to my father) antique farm tractors. Few categories can encompass such endless variety as costume jewelry.

Collectors of plastic seek Bakelite, Celluloid, Lucite, and regular old plastic. The tailored look can be satisfied with just about every designer and company. Wild for the ultra feminine look with lots of pearls and flowers? Say hello to Miriam Haskell. Does the wild and gaudy set your heart racing? Rhinestone creations by Eisenberg, Schreiner, Schiaparelli, and Juliana will satisfy that particular taste.

Price is always a consideration, no matter the collectible. It is one more great reason to collect costume jewelry. Many beautiful pieces are available for a dollar or two, less if you are a garage- or yardsaler. High-end Bakelite, Haskells, and Trifaris can sell for thousands of dollars. There is truly something for every collector.

With the advent of online auctions, it may seem easier than ever to build a collection. It could actually be harder. Collectors are seeking the best examples to add to their collections. Even though there are a great many pieces being offered, the best now usually go for high prices. If you want anything Miriam Haskell, you will pay a premium for it. At any given time, there will be a dozen collectors sniping during the last few seconds of a sale. When I first found eBay, there were around 350 listings of costume jewelry every day. One could spend an hour in front of the computer and view every single listing. Today there are, on average, over 35,000 listings of costume jewelry; it is impossible to see them all.

This means that unless you want to play hit and miss, just looking at new listings or those ending soon, collectors will need to specialize. I have seven names I look for every day, my favorites in my price range. I adore the look and feel of Mazer Bros., the rarity of Calvaire and Claudette, and the fun and somewhat silly side of Hattie Carnegie. Most collectors I know specialize in some*one* or some*thing*. I know Christmas tree pin collectors, owl pin collectors, even a few flamingo pin collectors. Some want only Trifari, others seek "gaudy"; still other look exclusively for "weird" and/or "odd."

Staret Torch.

There are ways to add Haskells to your collection without breaking your piggybank, but you have to be creative. White jewelry has few collectors, therefore you might find white Haskells affordable. Here is another place education pays off. Not all Miriam Haskell jewelry was signed; if you learn everything you can about her style and design, you can discover treasures no one else has seen yet.

As you peruse this book, you will see many designers who have had limited exposure in other books. I like to find designers no one else is looking for; it cuts down on the competition! I am going to introduce you to the work of Claudette, Calvaire, and Les Bernard. You may know Volupté as the compact company, but now you will know it for its great line of jewelry.

I love collecting vintage ads as much for their beautiful artwork and design as for the jewelry they feature. Additionally, it is quite a thrill to run across an ad featuring a piece of jewelry residing in your own jewelry box. That has happened to me several times, and the thrill is the same each time. And how amazing is it to pay over $100.00 for a pin and earrings that sold for $7.50 a set in 1957? Ads do more than you might imagine, as you will see when you read the column about ads that is found later in the book. Oh, and ads look great framed in your boudoir, home office, or showcases. Finding vintage ads and vintage costume jewelry is easier today than ever.

Foreword

Hobé.

In 1997 there were a very few websites featuring vintage costume jewelry for sale. Today they are countless. Many of the best ones have been around for four or five years, a few even longer, and they offer more than just jewelry for sale. The best offer historical information, ads, even tips on restoring and repairing vintage jewelry.

Some, such as Pat Seal's Reasearching Costume Jewelry, found at Dottie Stringfield's website illusionjewels.com, offer jewelry for sale, but Pat's interest in the background of the jewelry, the designer who first sketched it, and the company who manufactured it makes her a costume jewelry historian. Fortunately for all of us, she willingly shares her information because she is a great believer in the education aspect of collecting. Pat Seal is not the only costume jewelry historian out there, but she is the one who has always made herself available to me. I have visited with Pat and her husband Glendon many times, and I always leave amazed that she has once again taught me something new.

In my travels, I see many methods of displaying costume jewelry. Kim Paff displays her copper jewelry on velvet necklace holders, her Bakelite bangles in a Lucite ice bucket, and her most important jewelry in a hurricane basket. This is the basket she will grab in the event a hurricane heads up her stretch of beach. Nancy Canãs has professional, glass-topped, stackable cases. Georgia Robinson has dental cabinets with many drawers that allow for great organization.

I use those parts cabinets that you find in hardware stores. They are metal, so they can be stacked without fear of them tumbling. They have clear drawers with adjustable dividers. I use a black Sharpie marker to write the designer or company name on the front of the drawer, and believe it or not, the names are in alphabetical order. Of course, my current favorites reside in a divided drawer in my vanity, and I have jewelry boxes all over the place. One consequence of collecting costume jewelry is that you *must* have a variety of accessories to make the collection complete. I love old jewelry boxes, compacts, hatboxes, glove boxes, ring holders, even vintage fashions. And anything Schiaparelli.

One of the wonderful collectors who allowed me to photograph her jewelry was Patti Collins Bultman. What a fascinating day. Patti was the jewelry buyer for a boutique in the 1950s, and lived the dream of all of today's collectors. She got to go into the showrooms of the major jewelry companies to select the jewelry her boutique would carry. This one-time member of The Charmettes entertained us with singing ("Do the Hucklebuck!") and dancing, and the truth about how boring (oh, say it isn't so!) it was to sit at the Trifari showrooms and wait and wait and wait for them to bring a tray for her to choose from, and then wait and wait and wait for them to bring another tray for her, but no, she couldn't have any of *that* tray, it was reserved for another buyer with an exclusive.

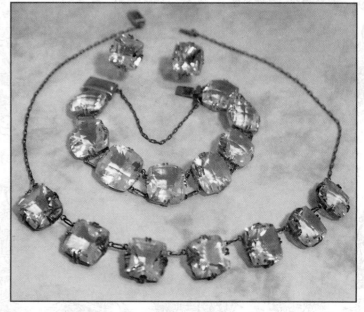

And what about the Haskell showrooms? Miriam Haskell made it a point to be briefly available to the buyers for a quick chat or an introduction.

Robert Mandle was Patti's personal friend, and made special items just for her. She told us that Mandle traveled to Europe, bought fetching little pieces of fine jewelry, then brought them home and used them for inspiration. Mandle gave some of these fine jewels to Patti when he was finished with them. I hope you enjoy seeing some of his exceptional creations. It was wonderful to hear her stories and learn about costume jewelry from a different point of view.

I rarely wear any of my collection when I go shopping for vintage costume jewelry. I like to question the dealers about their jewelry to see what I can learn from them. Many times they see me as a novice and willingly share their knowledge. I have found that when I go shopping loaded with costume jewelry they are not so willing to chat and bargain. But I have friends who *do* go out loaded up, because they like to see who they will meet because they are wearing the vintage costume jewelry.

This book is based on my column *Inside the Jewelry Box,* which appears monthly in selected antiques publications. All of the chapters are columns I have written over the past six years. I have done an enormous amount of reading and research over the years, and a considerable amount of knowledge has been gleaned from other jewelry books. My thanks go to all of those authors; I hope they had as much fun writing their books as I did this one. I want you to have fun when you are reading it; I hope I have shared something with you that you didn't know before you read my book. Don't take collecting too seriously; after all, it is supposed to be fun. And if you have something to tell me, email me at my website www.insidethejewelrybox.com, or at annmpitman@yahoo.com, or write to me in care of Collector Books.

Vintage costume jewelry collecting can reveal a whole new world for you. If you get lucky, you will make lifelong friends. One can never have enough jewelry or enough friends.

Coro sterling.

Mask pins.

Flamingo pins.

Introduction

The Beginning, Feburary 1997

Welcome to the new column, Inside the Jewelry Box. This column will be dedicated to costume jewelry; antique, vintage and even some contemporary. We'll be discussing designers, reproductions, what's hot, what's not, repairing, storing, buying tips, book reviews and we might even slip in some gossip!

Some people attribute the term "costume jewelry" to Coco Chanel, who designed pieces of jewelry to go with her current fashions. The jewelry could be disposed of when the fashion went out of style, according to Chanel. Others attribute it to Florence Ziegfeld who ordered jewelry to match his showgirls' costumes in the Ziegfeld Follies. Though both of these are highly entertaining, neither one is actually true. Harrice Simons Miller's book, "Costume Jewelry" reproduces an ad for the Ostby & Barton Company from 1917 that offers a look at the "new costume jewelry." It explains that "a woman with a flair for costume" now has accessories to go with it. It could just be the advertising agent's term.

Sparkle bracelet, celluloid with blue rhinestones; these are becoming more popular every day, and prices are rapidly increasing for the more interesting or more beautifully designed. **$200.00 – 250.00.** Author collection

I'm Ann Pitman, when I moved in 10 years ago, my neighbor, Linda McKay, called to tell me she had signed for a package for me. I walked over to pick it up. Upon entering her kitchen, I froze. Her dining room table was absolutely covered with jewelry. My novice comment was "Wow! You sure have a lot of jewelry!" Her reply, "it's all for sale", hooked me instantly. My education began a few weeks later in a bookstore with Maryanne Dolan's *Collecting Rhinestone Colored Jewelry*.

Costume jewelry uses its siren call in many ways. Davida Baron of Freshmeadows, New York, as a little girl, watched her mother sit at her vanity table, take the jewelry box Davida thought held the "Queens' Jewelry" out, and choose that evenings accessories. Davida was allowed to sit on the bed and play with all the wonderful diamonds, rubies, emeralds and sapphires. Years later, when she found out it wasn't real, she wanted no part of it, even declining her mother's offer to give her the box.

Then one day while shopping in an antique store, she admired the owner's orange dangling pin, who offered her the pin for $69.00. Davida left the store without the pin, but its siren call was at work. She could not get the pin out of her mind. She called the store to find out if it was still available, it was, and that was the beginning of her collection. "I think of all those jewels I had my mother give to someone else... I could kick myself, but I also think I had to grow into this passion my own way. My appreciation for each and every piece I collect, or even give as a gift, is deeper because of the path I had to take to get to where I am now." Davida is the co-editor of the Glittering Times newsletter devoted to costume jewelry.

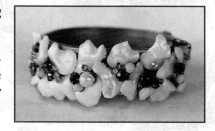

Susan Hagadorn of Somerville, Massachusetts is a brand new collector, who was "instantly hooked." Her passion is copper, and while surfing the Internet, she surfed into the site of Adornment, owned by Deb Schneider and discovered copper jewelry.

Marsha Harrison of Indianapolis, Indiana was dragged, kicking and screaming, well, kicking and complaining, along with her two sisters to a flea market. Marsha, a corporate attorney, visualizing booths filled with tube socks and tacky craft items, commented "Yuk!" Once they arrived, the second booth had a "pretty little art deco pin, with a big blue stone and gold tone wings. For some reason, I had to have it. And that was the beginning of the end. Now, seven years later, my bedroom, den and guest room are overflowing with costume jewelry." She even plans her clothing purchases to go with her jewelry. "I've concluded it's a disease," she emphatically states.

DeMario bangle bracelet, mother-of-pearl, jewel-tone rhinestones, clear rhinestones, and semi-precious cabochon stones, a gold gilt finish grosgrain ribbon interior. **$120.00 – 140.00.**
Kim Paff collection

Diana Schommer of Mars Hill, North Carolina suffered from "sister envy." She fell in love with a 1950s bracelet her sister had purchased in New York. It took her six months to find one for herself, and 2,500 pieces later, she still can't stop. Diana says she wears the jewelry constantly and mostly with jeans, because she loves the contrast. She occasionally sells pieces and her customers get a little something extra; "I always tell people how to care for the jewelry because I feel that it is an art form and if they take care of it, it will most likely grow in value."

Judi Scheele of Highland Village, Texas, has filled her online shop, A Wink and A Smile Vintage Designer Costume Jewelry and Accessories, with jewelry she acquired while "picking" vintage clothing for a friend in Seattle. Judi couldn't resist a piece of glitz, though her friend could. She found enough tailored 1930s and 1940s jewelry to keep her friend happy, but kept buying the glitz, until she had to open her own retail shop, three years ago. Now she has only antique mall showcases, and her website.

Not too far into the business, and not knowing anything about the jewelry she was attracted to, Judi made her first really wonderful jewelry "score," old Haskell, Hobé and Schreiner, all from one sale. She came straight home to begin researching what she had found, and "I was bitten by the bug. I wanted to spend all my time looking for jewels."

Janet Lawwill of Durango, Colorado, owner of the costume jewelry website Sparkles, has this tip for measuring cuffed, hinged and bangle bracelets: cut a flat 2-inch wide strip from around a 2 liter soda bottle. Lay it flat next to a ruler and mark the inches with a fine tip permanent marking pen. Roll it up and pop it inside the bracelet, uncoiled to the fullest extent, and you have the exact measurement.

Bib necklace and earring set from 1962, with prong-set glass rhinestones in Montana blue, pale pink, and pale blue. **$175.00 – 195.00.** Anne F. Ciotti collection

Every collector has their own story to tell, and each piece of costume jewelry just might have its own story to tell. We'll look for these stories in the coming months.

Staret bow brooch with clear rhinestones. **$250.00 – 300.00.** Nancy Canãs collection

Schiaparelli parure of antiqued silver-tone bracelet, brooch, and earrings with large pewter and black pearls and rhinestones. **$350.00 –500.00.**
Georgia Robinson collection

Miriam Haskell cross necklace with rhinestones, thirty inches long with a 3" cross. **$225.00 – 325.00+.**
Patti Collins Bultman collection

Boucher Raspberries, marked "Design Pat. Pend." Features different colored raspberries. 2½", circa 1939 – 1944. **$600.00 – 800.00.**
Laurel Ladd Ciotti collection

Castlecliff amber topaz cross pendent with a black center stone, 3½" x 2". **$95.00 – 115.00.**
Charlene Russ collection

Signed earrings with matching unsigned bracelet, Original by Robert, pink pearls, baroque pearls, and glass beads with AB rhinestones. **$220.00 – 250.00.**
Kim Paff collection

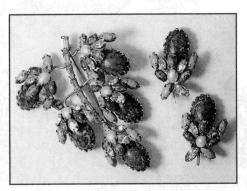

Schreiner brooch and earrings set, stylized floral spray with large faux coral and turquoise stones. **$300.00 – 375.00.** Georgia Robinson collection

Chanel parure with cross design, gold plated with a matt finish, includes two pairs of earrings, a charm bracelet, and a necklace. Marked "Chanel," "Made in France," and "1994." **$1,500.00 – 2,500.00** Nancy Canãs collection

Pair of penguins, jelly belly style with reverse carving , each almost 3". **$235.00 – 265.00** pair. Laurel Ladd Ciotti collection

Mazer Brothers

Joseph Mazer box with Mazer jewels. Author collection

Mazer Brothers jewelry is some of the most beautiful jewelry collectors can acquire. It is so finely crafted and elegantly designed that it is often mistaken for the "real" thing. The brothers Joseph and Lincoln, two of seven brothers who immigrated to the United States from Russia with their family in the mid-1920s, began Mazer Bros. in 1939. They staked their business reputation on the mimicry of genuine jewelry.

Joanne Dubbs Ball, author of *Costume Jewelers, The Golden Age of Design,* relates how the two started a shoe buckle business that had them converting low-heeled shoes to high-heeled ones, and adding fashionable buckles. Two associates who recognized the brother's talent were a stone importer, who supplied their buckle business and fellow costume jewelry designer Marcel Boucher. Both encouraged the Mazer Brothers to step out into jewelry design.

Many of the company's designs were inspired by the jewelry collections of royalty. One of the most famous Mazer Bros. designs is the Royal Orb pin. This brooch was designed around 1953, according to Cherri Simonds, author of *Collectible Costume Jewelry,* who features it in her chapter on brooches and pins. Simonds tells us that the pin was designed to celebrate the coronation of Queen Elizabeth II. This three inch brooch has a large gold orb as the bottom centerpiece with a row of large, deeply colored rhinestones in sapphire, Burmese ruby and emerald. The top piece is a Maltese cross with a sapphire blue rhinestone in the center, and the cross rests on an amethyst glass cabochon. Clear rhinestones crown the top of the orb. At first glance, it appears to be genuine stones and real gold. Simonds value is listed at five hundred to six hundred dollars.

The Mazer Brothers are also famous for a series of mask pins. These pins feature faces of clear pave' rhinestones, with colored rhinestones acting as the accents to each piece. The masks are apparently so well loved by collectors that they rarely show up for sale. Angie Gordon values them at three hundred to six hundred dollars each in her book, Twentieth Century Costume Jewelry.

Fur clips with emerald green and clear rhinestones, 2". **$295.00 – 325.00** pair. Laurel Ladd Ciotti collection

Jomaz fawn with turquoise body. **$40.00.** Laurel Ladd Ciotti collection

Joseph and Lincoln continued operating Mazer Brothers until shortly after World War II, when they begin producing separating lines, with the jewelry marked either "Mazer" or "Jomaz."

Collectors can usually recognize Mazer Bros. jewelry before they turn it over to look for a mark. The stones are brilliantly colored, the designs are timeless and classic, and each piece is manufactured with attention to detail. The backs of bracelets are well made and smooth to the touch, making them very comfortable to wear. The stones in my clear Mazer Bros. bracelet appear to be brand new, so brightly do they shine.

Blue floral spray, riveted back, 3", all the blue stones are unfoiled and open backed. I have seen the matching bracelet; it was as stunning as this brooch. Faintly marked with the top half of "MAZER." This set was also available in red. Rare. **$350.00 – 400.00.** Author collection

Back view of blue floral spray.

Flower-shaped fur clip with green and clear rhinestones, showing its age. **$25.00 – 40.00.** Author collection

Extraordinary green and clear bracelet in gold tone, with safety chain, 7" long. This beauty with the deepest of green stones lies perfectly on your wrist and could compete with one made of genuine stones. Note the fold over clasp has four rhinestones, a Mazer standard. Green center design stones are open backed. Beautifully handcrafted, a rare find in this color and condition. Marked "MAZER" on back of centerpiece. **$450.00 – 500.00.** Author collection

Mazer Brothers

Sky blue and clear bracelet with elaborate center-piece, requiring two rivets, stones are still very much alive considering the age of this piece. These style bracelets are hard to find in colors, easier in just clear stones. Their comfort when worn tells you Mazer paid as much attention to the design of the back as it did the front. Marked "MAZER BROS." on clasp. **$450.00 – 500.00.** Author collection

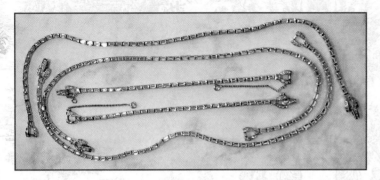

A variety of necklaces and bracelets in clear baguette stones, I have found this design in a narrow width and a wide width. The narrow has all baguettes, the wide has emerald and square cut stones, their incredible beauty can only be appreciated up close and personal. All clasps are marked MAZER BROS., some include the copyright symbol. Bracelets **$75.00 – 100.00,** necklaces **$125.00 – 150.00.** Author collection

Same style in a wide design with emerald and square stones, marked same as narrow. **$150.00 – 200.00.** Author collection

Three chokers, in red, green, and blue, 14", difficult to find. **$175.00 – 200.00** each, **$800.00+** set. Author collection

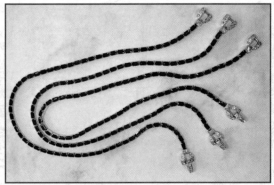

Pale lavender choker and bracelet, color rarely seen, absolutely beautiful in person. **$300.00 – 450.00** set. Author collection

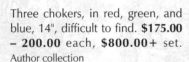

Because all of these necklaces and bracelets have the same clasp, they can be attached to one another to lengthen any necklace to a fit comfortable to today's collectors. The fancy clasps can hang in the front or the back. Author collection

Narrow sky blue bracelet, 7½". **$95.00 – 125.00.** Author collection

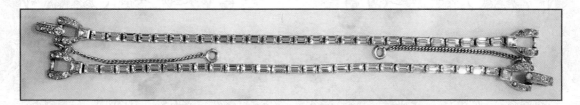

Narrow clear bracelets. **$75.00 – 100.00.** Author collection

Wide ruby red bracelet; emerald-shape stones are actually slightly lighter than square stones; 7½", the only one I have seen in 12 years. **$350.00 – 450.00.** Author collection

Jomaz brooch with large lapis center stone, open in the back. **$25.00 – 30.00.** Author collection

Jomaz black enameled toothy whale, 2". **$50.00 – 75.00.** Author collection

Lavender bird with long fluid tail feathers, riveted wings, almost 4". **$200.00 – 250.00.** Author collection

Large pink center stone sets off this set with matching earrings; all pieces marked "MAZER BROS.," clasp design is slightly different. **$100.00 – 150.00** set. Author collection

Calvaire

Years ago I found the most beautiful brooch that appeared to have genuine amethyst stones in it. The back of the pin was marked Calvaire, and closer inspection revealed that the amethyst stones were glass and the little diamonds were rhinestones. The back of the pin shows the high level of quality of the company that made the jewelry. I have spent five years looking for more information on Calvaire to no avail. The only information I have been able to find is that the company was a French company doing business in France and the United States. They were in business from sometime in the 1920s through sometime in the 1960s, judging from the design of the jewelry.

In looking at their jewelry, and the accessories I have been able to find, I suspect it was a French company that made women's accessories. I have found jewelry, compacts and handbags with the same mark in them. Every piece of Calvaire jewelry I own is Sterling, therefore it was likely available in high end boutiques, jewelry departments and jewelry stores.

There is a wealth of information about jewelry designers and companies on the website, www.illusionjewels.com, which is owned by Dotty and George Stringfield and which hosts Pat Seal's Researching Costume Jewelry. Stringfield and Seal are both costume jewelry historians. They have compiled a work-in-progress that includes company names, dates of operation, and if available, the company mark. Their information, compiled from several costume jewelry references states that Calvaire was founded by Ray Calish, an importer and manufacturer of costume jewelry.

I believe more can be determined about this company as more of their jewelry and accessories are found. The pages following show nearly every item in my collection. I have been actively seeking Calvaire jewelry for a decade, and have found less than a dozen pieces. Even with the Internet, it is almost impossible to find this jewelry. It is so rare, only four or five pieces come up for Internet auctions each year. My research continues.

Stunning amethyst flower pin, with open unfoiled amethyst stones, and white baguettes, 4½" x 2½", marked "CALVAIRE." The C is somewhat larger, allowing the *alvaire* to be placed on the bottom "leg" of it. Rare, very rare. **$550.00 – 600.00.** Author collection

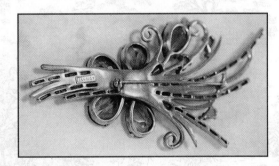

Back view of amethyst flower pin.

Large Calvaire sterling bracelet with 1" blue unfoiled open-back glass stones. Gold wash over sterling, safety chain, 7½" x ¾", the only Calvaire bracelet I have seen in 12 years. Also very rare. **$500.00 – 600.00.** Author collection

Calvaire sterling flower, with green and amethyst rhinestones, gold wash, 4" x 2". Very rare. **$450.00 – 500.00.** Author collection

Reverse view of flower with green stones.

Calvaire sterling pansy fur clip, gold wash, 2" x 1¾", fair condition. **$100.00 – 125.00.** Author collection

Calvaire compact, nearly 3", top is covered with large rhinestones, a few quite dull. **$50.00 – 80.00.** Author collection

Calvaire sterling earrings, either a butterfly or another flying insect, enamel and rhinestones, clip on, 1¾" x 1½", both earrings are marked. Rare. **$200.00 – 250.00.** Author collection

Reverse view of earring.

Tiny Calvaire vanity purse, expanding gate clasp, marked "Made in France" on back of gate, tag inside reads "MADE IN FRANCE Especially for CALVAIRE NEW YORK." Rare. **$300.00 – 350.00.** Author collection

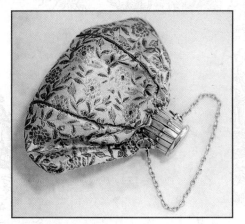

View of opened purse .

Claudette

My research for Claudette has been as unfruitful as that of Calvaire. The Claudette name was owned by Premier Jewelry Company Inc, of New York, and they first used the mark in 1945. That is the extent of the information available. As with Calvaire, we may be able to determine more about the company by the jewelry they produced.

There are basically three classifications of Claudette. First is the bold, over the top designs that may be mistaken for Juliana designs. These use some of the same stones, with some of the same unusual combinations. And big, these jewels are big. The back of the jewelry is either japanned black or a plain matte finish I call gunmetal. The earrings are always marked, the pins are never marked. I have seen matching bracelets that were unmarked. I have seen matching necklaces both marked and unmarked.

Red trefoil or clover design, set of pin and earrings, 2½", japanned black, impossible to get a photograph to show how beautiful the Claudette pieces are in person. Only the earrings are marked. Rare. **$300.00 – 325.00** set. Author collection

Next is the mild design division. These pieces have quieter designs with a smaller size overall. The back of the jewelry is usually gold tone or silver tone with a high rhodium gloss finish. Some pieces have been found with an antiqued gold finish. The earrings are marked, the pins are not. I have not seen bracelets or necklaces to match, but if they are not signed, it would be almost impossible to find any.

Last is the thermoplastic division. These designs are easy to find, they came in a variety of colors, and complete parures are readily found or accrued. Nearly every piece is marked on the back of the jewelry holding the "first" piece of thermoplastic in the design. Though these do not appeal to me, they do have a devoted following.

Claudette jewelry has two signatures, the first, found on the back of the bold earrings, is a large all caps signature that circles the top of the ear clip. The second, found on the quieter pieces is a small tight straight line signature of all caps. The same signature is found on the thermoplastic line. It leaves me wondering ... were there two different companies using the Claudette signature?

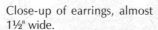

Close-up of red pin.

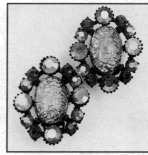

Close-up of earrings, almost 1½" wide.

Blue snowflake-shaped pin and earrings, japanned, almost 2½", only earrings marked. Rare. **$300.00 – 325.00** set. Author collection

Close-up of blue pin.

Reverse view of pin.

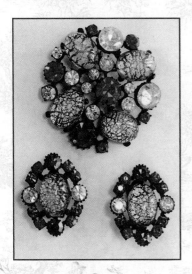

Fall colors set with hyacinth stones, pin is 2¼", only earrings marked, japanned. **$250.00 – 300.00.** Author collection

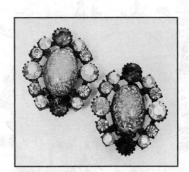

Close-up of blue earrings.

Claudette

Lavender and red pinwheel set of pin and earrings; note center piece of pin is identical to earrings; pin is almost 2", earrings are over 1", on original card, earrings marked. **$275.00 – 300.00** set.
Author collection

Close-up of pin.

Back of red pinwheel pin.

Close-up of earrings.

Back of earrings with signature.

Blue and green set with green cabochons, rhodium plated, 2½", has bale for hanging from a chain, earrings 1", only earrings are marked. I have also seen this set in all blue stones. **$125.00 – 150.00** set. Author collection

Close-up of pin.

Large round red pin and earrings, some aurora borealis stones, pin is 2¼", gunmetal back, earrings are 1¼", only earrings are marked. **$275.00 – 300.00** set. Author collection

Close-up of earrings.

Different-style pinwheel set of red and pink rhinestones, 2", gunmetal back, earrings are almost 1½", only earrings are marked. **$225.00 – 250.00** set. Author collection

Different photo of set.

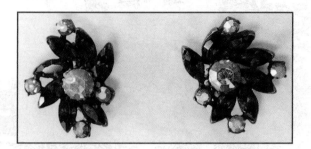

Close-up of earrings.

Stylized star pin in red and purple stones, gun-metal back, 3"; not marked, but clearly Claudette. **$100.00 – 125.00.** Author collection

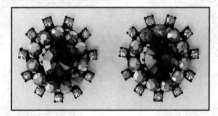

Dark red and pink pinwheel earrings, japanned, 1", marked "Claudette." **$60.00 – 75.00.** Author collection

Green and pale blue earrings, 1¼", gunmetal back. **$60.00 – 75.00.** Author collection

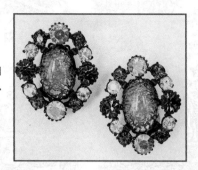

Green oval earrings, japanned; I can't wait to find the pin that matches these. **$75.00 – 85.00.** Author collection

Pastel set of pin and earrings, gold tone, pin is nearly 2", earrings are almost 1", beautiful colors, quiet design, completely different from other Claudette jewels, only earrings are marked. **$50.00 – 75.00** set. Author collection

Clear aurora borealis rhinestone earrings, 1¼", gold tone, signed "Claudette," signature identical to art glass sets above. **$25.00 – 35.00.** Author collection

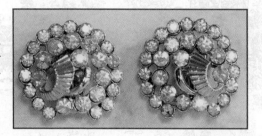

Back view of earring with signature.

Antiqued gold purple clip earrings, different Claudette signature, over 1½". **$45.00 – 50.00.** Author collection

Pale blue rhinestone starfish pin, almost 2", rhodium plated, on original card. **$45.00 – 50.00.** Author collection

Blue rhinestone and pearl earrings, 1½", rhodium plated, signed. **$25.00 – 30.00.** Author collection

Red thermoplastic Claudette necklace, signed, 15". **$35.00 – 50.00.** Author collection

This fall colors set has shades of brown rhinestones, some in aurora borealis finish. This parure includes bracelet, pin, and earrings; the earrings and bracelet are marked, the pin is not. **$155.00 – 175.00.** Treasures-in-Time-collection

Bracelet.

Earrings.

Pin.

House of de Lillo

The costume jewelry world is seemingly filled with millions of designs in every imaginable range of style, quality, material and color. But when you see a piece of jewelry by the firm of William de Lillo Ltd. you know you are holding a stylish piece of quality art.

Dark blue tassel necklace, 32", with an additional 6" of tassel. Marked "deLillo" on back of clasp, **$175.00 – 200.00.** Author collection

Art? Yes, art. Robert F. Clark and William de Lillo formed the company known as William de Lillo Ltd. in the late 1960s and were equal partners from the beginning. But art? Yes, art.

Robert F. Clark is a designer extraordinaire. He was the chief designer and vice president of Miriam Haskell, where he worked for ten years. William de Lillo was designing for such prestigious companies as Tiffany, Cartier and Winston. These exceptional talents met, became best friends, formed their company and collaborated to bring something special to the costume jewelry world.

I recently had the opportunity to speak with Mr. de Lillo and I admit I was star struck. I rarely have the chance to speak with someone whose jewelry I own and admire. He shared insight of why so little de Lillo jewelry comes on the marketplace now and why prices are so high when it does appear.

"We catered to an elite clientele. They had everything and never had enough. These elite women had a tremendous wardrobe and wanted fashionable pieces to add to their wardrobe," de Lillo stated.

He continued, "We designed four large collections per year. The designs were then put away, never to be produced again. The collections were shown to the buyers by appointment in our own showrooms. . . . We made only what was ordered. We were never a volume house."

"Bob Clark designed most of our jewelry. It was hand made and hand set," de Lillo says of the quality. "We were known for quality and we brought something different to the marketplace. All production was executed through our loyal staff of workers in our own workrooms." He says further, "Concerning the creation of our four yearly collections in New York and later in Paris, Clark and I have always had a close artistic collaboration."
Clark and de Lillo designed costume jewelry throughout the 1960s and 1970s.

Author Ginger Moro states in her book *European Designer Jewelry* that Clark and de Lillo lived and worked in France from 1976 until 1986. Mr. de Lillo told me that he and Mr. Clark worked in sculpture jewelry in the 1980s, working with real gold and silver, but now they are living in Arizona and creating only sculpture. Art? Yes, art.

FYI: Do you have the book *The Jewels of Miriam Haskell* by Deanna Farneti Cera? Mr. de Lillo gave me a list of page numbers where designs were incorrectly attributed. If you have this book you might like to read more about Robert F. Clark and make the appropriate corrections. The following pages should be attributed to Robert F. Clark: 23, 37, 104, 105, 126, 127, 130, 134, and 142. Also, the necklace on page 198 was designed by Bob Clark.

Turquoise nugget style necklace, 28", with a pendent drop of 4". Necklace has a deLillo hang tag. **$150.00 – 175.00.** Author collection

Turquoise blue button earrings, clip on, ⅞". **$25.00 – 45.00.** Author collection

Black dangle earrings, elegant and lightweight, black drop is lightweight plastic, almost 2½". **$80.00 – 100.00.** Author collection

Star stickpin, notice markings on clasp, 3". **$75.00 – 100.00.** Author collection

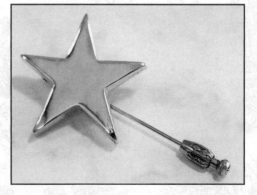

Mark of deLillo.

Egyptian-influenced necklace and bracelet with turquoise beads and gold color separators. Necklace is 15¾". Bracelet is 7". **$225.00 – 295.00.** Treasures-in-Time collection

Crystal cross with bevel-cut crystal rectangle links surrounded by prong-set clear rhinestones, gold over white metal setting; cross is 2⅛", the chain is 31", signed on clasp. Designed by Robert Clark. **$595.00 – 675.00.** Treasures-in-Time collection

This Lucite crystal-studded cross is an enormous 5" x 5", with square Lucite crystals and a large center Lucite stone; the cross has a 32" chain set with faux pearls. Signed on the back of the cross and on the chain. **$585.00 – 650.00.** Treasures-in-Time collection

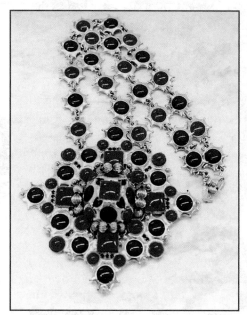

Red and blue medallion necklace and earrings set on silver tone metal, the medallion is 4½" on a 21" chain. Only the earrings are marked "deLillo NY," in block letters. **$795.00 – 895.00.** Treasures-in-Time collection

Lucite brooch made with four pairs of faceted Lucite flutes; the center is wired with Lucite faceted beads and rhinestone chain; gold-plated metal, 4¼", signed "Wm DeLillo" in script on an applied oval on the back. **$465.00 – 550.00.** Treasures-in-Time collection

Clear Lucite choker with nineteen clear Lucite faceted flutes attached to gold-plated openwork neck-piece, signed "DeLillo" in script on an oval hanging tag, measures 15" with the extender. **$535.00 – 625.00.** Treasures-in-Time collection

Hattie Carnegie

The Kanengeiser family emigrates from Austria to the United States at the beginning of the new century, looking for a better life, and a brighter future. They bring with them little Henrietta, and begin their new life on New York's Lower East Side. Mr. Kanengeiser dies shortly after their arrival, and little Henrietta drops out of school to go to work and help her mother support the family.

One of her first jobs is as a messenger for Macy's department store. She soon moves into the millinery workroom as a model, and Henrietta also works as a pin girl in a dress house. In her spare time she designs hats for neighborhood ladies. Here is where the typical immigrant's story begins to change.

First she changes her name to that of the richest man in America at that time, she becomes Hattie Carnegie, and opens a small custom clothing shop. With her friend and partner Rose Roth doing the sewing and a clientele including Mrs. Randolph Hearst, the shop is on it's way to becoming a success. Rose makes the dresses and Hattie makes the hats and waits on the customers. Soon the diminutive Hattie, only four feet ten inches tall, is sole owner, and she moves her business to a townhouse on East 49th Street, off Park Avenue.

Hattie has a great sense of style, a flair for fashion and great business acumen. She begins making buying trips to Europe, eventually going four times each year, and bringing back the latest styles, which she adapts and improves, with American flair. She is seen all over New York, her own best advertisement, in her own designs, with her accessories, her jewelry and her own perfumes, all of which soon become famous. Her clientele now includes the Duchess of Windsor, society beauties, and stage and movie stars such as Joan Crawford, Constance Bennett, and Tallulah Bankhead.

The 1930s were tough for the fashion and jewelry industries, but Hattie comes through with a ready-to-wear department. In the early 1950s she designs the habits for the Carmelite Sisters "Society of Christ", the Women's Army Corps uniforms, and those for the Army Nurse Corps and the Women's Medical Specialist Corps. These designs for the Army earn her the Army's highest civilian award, and a glance at today's uniforms still bear out her design influence.

After 59 years in the fashion industry, having achieved the promise of her bright future, Hattie Carnegie died at age 70 in 1956. Her salon continued until 1965, and her jewelry and perfume continued to be produced until the 1970s. Her jewelry designs were never intended to be copies of genuine fine jewelry. Instead she liberally used materials such as plastic, and rhinestones were used merely as enhancements to each piece. Her highly collectible early jewelry with the Hattie Carnegie signature is expensive when available, but it is difficult to find. It was very costly when made and sold by Hattie, and the prices continue to climb steadily.

Hattie Carnegie jewelry was made from 1918 until 1970. The marks of her jewelry include:

"Hattie" above "Carnegie," in a thick, slanted script,
"Hattie Carnegie," in a thin, less-slanted script,
"Carnegie" alone,
"Hattie" above "Carnegie," in or on an oval disk
"Double Exposure," her mark for earrings,
 possibly an "HC" in a diamond,
"Miss Hattie,"
and "Pooped Pussy Cat" and "Pooped Poodle," which are found on hair ornaments, jeweled shoe buckles,
 jeweled cases, and jeweled holders.

Hattie believed that women dressed to please men, but she designed her clothes to suit the woman. When a woman wearing one of her designs walked into a room, Hattie wanted people to say, "What a beautiful woman!" instead of "What a beautiful dress." A classic Hattie comment: "It's much better to wear clothes that are too young for you than clothes designed for an old woman."

In 1945, Hattie Carnegie's dress business was making $6,500,000.00 each year, her high end dresses sold for $79.00 to $125.00. She designed her clothes in sizes 8 to 40, but allowances were made and patterns slightly changed to tone down details unsuitable to larger size women.

Her whole family, including nieces and nephews worked for her company. In 1945, she sold furs, costume jewelry, chocolate bonbons, cosmetics, bags, slips, bed jackets, blouses, slacks, perfumes and scarves, in addition to dresses and hats. There was no logic to what she sold in her stores, if she liked it, she carried it, and in the case of the bonbons, she found a good recipe in Paris and put it to good use.

Her retail shop was several stories high, and the higher you went, the higher the prices went. Ladies on the top floor were willing to pay at least $195.00 for a custom made dress. Each customer had her own regular salesgirl, who had her own desk. Once you became a good enough customer, you achieved "dummy" distinction; a dummy with your measurements was made and kept in the workrooms. Ladies would sit on sofas and chaises while models paraded around the showroom dressed in Hattie's latest offerings.

When Hattie made shopping trips to Europe, she would welcome salesmen to her bathroom in her suite at the Ritz hotel, and would spend the time sitting in her bubble bath viewing the day's offerings of buttons, fabrics and bags.

Hattie Carnegie sitting at her desk.
Life Magazine — November 12, 1945

Hattie wore her own clothes right out of her store, and almost always sold them right off her back, to be delivered of course, after she returned from the Opera or a play and had them dry cleaned. One customer called, and asked for a mink coat she had finally made up her mind to purchase, only to be told Hattie had worn it to lunch, but she could have it when Hattie returned.

Hattie's greatest hobbies? Gin rummy and slot machines.

Hattie Carnegie is buried in the Ferncliff Cemetery in Hartsdale, New York alongside such notables as Judy Garland, Basil Rathbone, Malcolm X, and one of her customers, Joan Crawford.

Miss Carnegie Advises Mrs. Lawrence Tibbett (seated), who wants a new dress for the opera. Josephine Hughes, Hattie's assistant, sits at right.
Life magazine — November 12, 1945

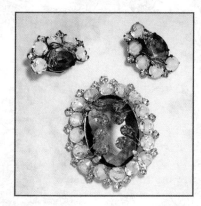

Green art glass bracelet and earrings; stones are open in back, bracelet is 7" long and is marked on a plaque on the back of one of the large stones, earrings are 1¼ " long, only one is marked. **$130.00 – 150.00.** Author collection

Topaz pin and earring set, large center stone is "held" in place by carved amber leaves. **$125.00 – 150.00.** Georgia Robinson collection

Close-up of topaz pin.

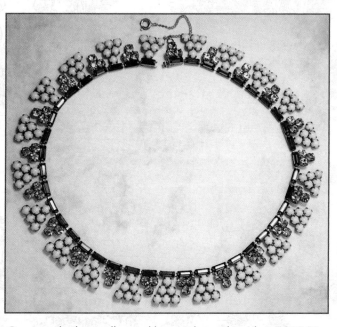

Green and white collar necklace with a safety chain. **$95.00 – 125.00.** Georgia Robinson collection

Original Hattie Carnegie jewelry tag. Author collection

Happy fisherman pin holds flowers and fish, attached with screws, very rare. Part of an Oriental design series. **$350.00 – 400.00.**
Author collection

Back of happy fisherman pin.

White mother-of-pearl japanned pin with clear rhinestones. **$75.00 – 100.00.**
Georgia Robinson collection

Three-dimensional pear pin. **$95.00 – 115.00.**
Georgia Robinson collection

Abstract green star brooch with glass stones. **$95.00 – 115.00.**
Georgia Robinson collection

Red cabochon, green and blue stone clip-on earrings. **$45.00 – 60.00.**
Georgia Robinson collection

Crescent pin with wire-wrapped reddish purple stones, accented with clear round stones. **$85.00 – 115.00.**
Georgia Robinson collection

Red glass bead necklace with matching earrings. A previous owner took this once two-strand necklace and made it one long strand, removing the marked clasp in the process. If original, **$150.00 – 175.00** for the set; as-is, **$100.00.** Author collection

Mesh necklace and bracelet set, very tailored look, with clear stones, necklace is 14½" long, bracelet 6¾" long. **$100.00 – 125.00.**
Georgia Robinson collection

Donkey with flower cart, glass flower shaped beads; this little donkey was available with several designs of beads and flowers in his little cart. **$150.00 – 175.00.** Author collection

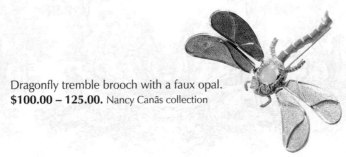

Dragonfly tremble brooch with a faux opal. **$100.00 – 125.00.** Nancy Canās collection

Cabochon bracelet and earrings in shades of blue and green, quite eye-catching when worn. **$200.00 – 250.00.** Nancy Canās collection

Blue-green pin and earrings with blue watermelon stones; the pin is 2¾" tall, the earrings are 1½". **$135.00 – 165.00.** Treasures-in-Time collection

Bib necklace in gold tone with dark blue and green plastic teardrop beads; the large medallion shapes feature round and marquise green and blue rhinestones, signed in script on an applied oval on the back of the clasp. The medallion pieces are 3" long and 2½" wide; the necklace is 23" long. **$595.00 – 675.00.** Treasures-in-Time collection

Pin and earrings set with multicolor rhinestones and faux pearls in a closed-back shiny gold setting, large center green rhinestone is open back, 2½" x 2"; earrings are 1½" x 1¼". **$215.00 – 240.00.** Treasures-in-Time collection

Beautifully-designed pin with clear and red rhinestones, and large red teardrop. **$95.00 – 120.00.** Treasures-in-Time collection

Nettie Rosenstein

When I first started collecting costume jewelry, I didn't know anything about it, except that I loved the colorful little sparklers. I shopped around, blissfully unaware there could be such a thing as a signature on the back. It was quite a shock to discover that a piece I coveted was totally unattainable price-wise because of a name on the back of the pin.

I remember it well, clear and bright yellow rhinestones made up the three-inch "horse's" head, emerald green eyes of course, and the mane was danglers of clear stones. No, I don't collect horse jewelry (though I do have a beauty of a running horse pin in gold tone with a rhinestone mane). But this horse pin, it spoke to me, no, it SHOUTED at me, "you must take me home!" "OK!" I shouted back to it, and reached for my wallet while asking for it to be removed from the showcase.

Up to this time I had never paid more than $20.00 for a piece of costume jewelry. You can imagine my total shock and dismay to discover that this little beauty was $145.00. The clerk's response to my "but why?" was, "Oh, it's a Weiss pin." As if that explained it all. I said a sad goodbye to the little horse pin and headed straight to the library to figure out this dilemma.

Nearly sixteen years later, I have added over 50 jewelry books to my library, read them, studied them, even memorized parts of them. There are still a few names that surprise me, and some I don't recognize, but I have a clear understanding of

Heraldic medallion necklace of two angels holding a jeweled crown. **$200.00 – 250.00.** Georgia Robinson collection

why some costume jewelry is so expensive and some is so inexpensive.

Nettie Rosenstein is one of those names that was unattainable to me when I first started collecting jewelry. Most of her jewelry was Sterling, therefore the prices are higher than comparable pieces. However, since prices have spiraled downward in the last couple of years, I now own several examples of Nettie Rosenstein jewelry.

Sterling apple pendant, has dangling rhinestone accents all over the apple and pavéd leaves. **$300.00 – 325.00.** Author collection

Nettie Rosenstein was born in Vienna, Austria, just like Hattie Carnegie; like Carnegie, her family emigrated to the United States. And like Carnegie, Rosenstein changed her family name from its original of Rosencrans, according to Joann Dubbs Ball in "Costume Jewelry, The Golden Age of Design." Ball relates Rosenstein's history of beginning in millinery, then moving into clothing and accessory designing, including perfume, handbags and jewelry. For a brief period during her thirties, Rosenstein retired, but came back to the design world a few years later, and quickly built a multi million dollar empire.

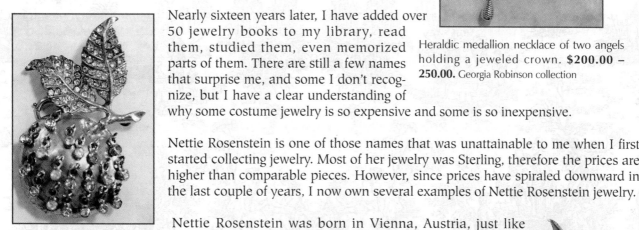

Rosenstein was a bit of a perfectionist, insisting on supervising every detail of production to manufacture the quality she demanded. And quality is it, even though it is not all desirable. Many of Rosenstein's jewelry designs revolved around heraldic jewelry, with designs of shields and medals, even coin jewelry. Not all collectors want this style today.

Back of apple dangle pendant.

Rosenstein produced enough other designs to keep us all happy. Her playful side was revealed in the animal line she designed; enameled and rhinestoned roosters, sweater pins of golden frogs, pearl bug brooches, even a stunning black Indian elephant head pendant.

Many of Rosenstein's designs rivaled genuine jewelry. Her flower basket pin looks like it contains sapphires, rubies and emeralds, though they are merely excellent rhinestones. Cherri Simonds's book, *Collectible Costume Jewelry*, features only one Nettie Rosenstein jewel, a watch fob brooch that has hand-painted enamel flowers, signed "H," in gold vermeil over sterling, mimicking genuine jewelry.

But Rosenstein didn't limit herself to jewelry. She started in millinery as a hat designer, gradually moving into designing clothes. During a visit to the National Museum of American History, I viewed an exhibit of First Ladies dresses, and remembered having seen a dress designed by Rosenstein. I contacted Susan Strange, the reference assistant in the Archives Center for more information. Strange spoke with Kate Henderson, who is responsible for the care of the First Ladies collection.

Apple charm bracelet; same design and style as the apple pendant on the preceding page, but is unmarked. **$100.00 – 120.00.** Author collection

Henderson shared the information that Mamie Eisenhower wore a rose-colored dress designed by Rosenstein to a state dinner. They also have on exhibit a beaded handbag designed by Rosenstein that Mamie carried at a 1953 inaugural event.

It's not very often that my family shows the slightest interest in my jewelry collection, except to tell me if something I am wearing is too big, and my husband checks me for a "tilt" factor, to make sure the large brooch is balanced by the gaudy bracelet. However, the day we left for Washington, the mail brought my first Nettie Rosenstein acquisition, an apple pendant, with leaves of rhinestones and little rhinestones dangling across the face of the apple.

As we stood in front of Mamie's dress, I fished in my purse for the apple pendant, and showed my husband and daughter that the apple was designed by the same lady who had designed a dress for a First Lady. They were mildly impressed, but I felt a sense of the history of costume jewelry, which I have never forgotten. Nettie Rosenstein died in 1980 at the age of ninety.

Green "baked potato" stone with large green rhinestones, with matching earrings. The dealer I bought this from in 1996 tried to purchase it back from me the following week for six times what I had paid her for it. She finally admitted that she had seen the complete parure at a show in Atlanta, Georgia, and only the necklace had been marked "Nettie Rosenstein." Without having seen it myself, I have priced it as a beautiful piece of unmarked jewelry; the value would at least double if it were truly Nettie Rosenstein. **$100.00 – 125.00.** Author collection

Juliana

The name JULIANA has recently caught fire in the costume jewelry collecting world. Until recently, few collectors had ever heard the name, and wouldn't have known a thing about it if they had, as no guidebook has ever covered Juliana.

Juliana jewelry can be explained in one simple word — gaudy. Not tacky, mind you, just gaudy. No other word can explain the unique combinations of stones set upon the links of Juliana construction. A few fortunate collectors found jewelry with the Juliana hang tag on it, in never-worn condition, and now collectors can put a possible name with a definite style.

Peacock in green stones, right down to his little feet. **$125.00 – 140.00.**
Laurel Ladd Ciotti collection

Bracelets are extremely easy to distinguish; earrings, brooches and necklaces less so. Once you understand the look of Juliana, it becomes easier to identify. First, each bracelet usually has five links, rectangular or oval, clearly seen from the back. Next, the clasp is etched, in a pattern similar to the feather of an arrow. Most bracelets have a safety chain.

Now for the stones. All types of beautiful and unusual rhinestones were used, and all shapes of stones. Art glass, carved stones, stones that look like opals, rivoli stones and watermelon stones. Even cameos. And most are large stones, surrounded by slightly smaller stones, accented by slightly smaller stones.

And that's not all. Many bracelets feature glass beads of all shapes and sizes, mounted into the top of the bracelet, above the large rhinestones, for a dangling, noisy, fun effect. These fabulous bracelets can be found with matching earrings, with the dangling beads, and brooches also accented with beads.

And the colors, well, the colors spark. Yes, some have pale colors, but most are bold. And some of the pale ones are accented with bold sparkled stones, in colors you dreamed could be worn together, but were too shy to try. Now collectors proudly model their Juliana.

Pamela Wiggins, a guide for About.com, http://antiques.about.com, explains, "The entire discovery of Juliana jewelry during the last year or so has been very interesting to watch. It seems that many people were attracted to this type of bracelet with ring and band construction and the matching items that go along with them, they just didn't know which company (or distributor) the quality and workmanship should be attributed."

Cheryl Killmer, Past Perfection Vintage Costume Jewelry (www.pastperfection.com) owns 450 to 500 pieces of Juliana, several which still have the original paper tag. "I love Juliana for its extravagant use of big, bold and colorful stones, and their interesting placement," said Killmer. Wiggins agrees, "Whoever made them during the late 1950s and early 1960s did a fantastic job of incorporating eye-catching stones into dramatic, colorful designs. It was just a matter of time until they were discovered and appreciated."

Lorie Mattson of Whiskey Creek Jewels (www.whiskey-creek.net/jewelry1.html) has a few pieces of treasured Juliana, but concentrates on the cameos, which come in an amazing array of color combinations. Mattson states, "As a collector I am ALWAYS looking for Juliana cameos, as they are hard to find and my goal is to see how many colors and combinations I can find. The fun is in the hunt!"

Because Juliana is unsigned, it was mostly overlooked, except by collectors who disregard marks and buy the jewelry by its appearance, manufacture and beauty. Past sellers had these unsigned charmers for as little as ten or twenty dollars, with sets priced at twenty five dollars and up. Now that it can be definitely attributed, prices have skyrocketed. Parures are bringing two, three and four hundred dollars while bracelets easily top one hundred dollars. Brooches can still be found reasonably priced, as they are harder to attribute. Necklaces, extremely difficult to attribute unless you have the rest of the matching set, stand on their own price-wise.

Stylized pink flowers bracelet. **$125.00 – 145.00.** Author collection

Will these prices come down? This collector hopes so, as she has always been into gaudy. Lorie Mattson says, "Like every other hot designer or style, the prices will come and go. Just as Hobé used to be so sought after, and is now in a slump. Does that make it less appealing or the quality lower? No, just a trend that is done for now, and may come back. In the last few years, everything was attributed to Weiss, because the Weiss name was being sought. Now if you look at the market, some of the same pieces that used to be attributed to Weiss (or Regency or Schreiner) are now being touted as Juliana!"

Pamela Wiggins doesn't "believe placing a name on these items has increased their desirability. It's still unsigned jewelry for the most part and no one's been able to pinpoint the origin, yet." She continues, "What makes it valuable is the beauty and craftsmanship. The real benefit of the name association is being able to easily identify the type of jewelry being sought. You can search for Juliana in an online auction instead of paging through oodles of unsigned jewelry hoping to find a piece here or there."

Collectors need to be cautioned that unaware or unscrupulous sellers may call their jewelry Juliana just to attain higher prices. By studying the construction of bracelets, and asking sellers for photos of the back of each piece, buyers can protect themselves.

Update: The spring issue of *Vintage Fashion & Costume Jewelry* magazine, available by subscription, profiled Frank De Lizza, whose father started the De Lizza and Elster Company, a jewelry manufacturer. He explained that De Lizza and Elster had manufactured the Juliana line for only two years, 1963 and 1964; it just wasn't a big seller. I asked him about the different names on the same

Back view of pink flowers bracelet.

jewelry, and he said the company had manufactured the Juliana line for other companies, which named the line Gloria and Tara. De Lizza and Elster was only a supplier to those companies. Mr. De Lizza stated that not all Julianas had safety chains, price was a factor, and that the company plated in all types of finishes — silver, black, Russian gold, and copper, to name a few. He explained that De Lizza and Elster had a design department that came up with all the designs, but all the principals provided direction.

Deep orange bracelet and earrings, **$145.00 – 175.00.** Author collection

My favorite Juliana set in green glass stones and beads; makes a joyful noise when you wear it; bracelet and earrings. **$165.00 – 200.00.** Author collection

Clear rhinestones and beads make up this Juliana pin. You have to see the matching bracelet to know it is a Juliana, and I have. **$40.00 – 45.00.** Author collection

Pale pink stones bracelet, relatively small for a Juliana. **$75.00 – 95.00.** Author collection

Montana blue rhinestones and pearl dangles, in silver tone. **$125.00 – 140.00.** Georgia Robinson collection

This bracelet and earrings set in red speckled art glass is one of the most sought after designs. **$250.00 – 300.00.** Georgia Robinson collection

Speckled art glass bracelet in greens and gold, with matching earrings. **$225.00 – 250.00.** Treasures-in-Time collection

Earrings.

Pale lavenders make up this bracelet with long teardrop-shaped stones. **$150.00 – 195.00.** Treasures-in-Time collection

Pink, blue, and white stones, clear and opaque; bracelet. **$120.00 – 140.00.** Treasures-in-Time collection

Matching brooch in blues, with pink stone accents and white center. **$125.00 – 140.00.**
Treasures-in-Time collection

Shades-of-aqua bracelet. **$135.00 – 175.00.** Treasures-in-Time collection

Yellow and brown marbled set of pin and earrings. **$95.00 – 120.00.**
Treasures-in-Time collection

Les Bernard

Les Bernard Jewelry Company originally was founded in 1936 under the name of Vogue, and became Les Bernard in 1963. The name is a combination of the partners Bernard Shapiro and Lester Joy. They closed up shop in 1996.

Les Bernard was extremely inventive, combining materials and design styles previously unheard of in jewelry manufacturing. One of their registered trademarked innovations was a process called "Diamond Point Texture" according to the book *Masterpieces of Costume Jewelry* by Joanne Dubbs Ball and Dorothy Hehl Torem. They show an example of a prancing horse, whose entire body is covered with tiny indentations made by a diamond-pointed tool. The horse has genuine ruby eyes, another Les Bernard innovation. Many of their designs feature genuine precious and semi-precious stones.

Another Les Bernard concept is the use of marcasites and rhinestones in the same piece of jewelry, previously unheard of because of the difficulty in manufacturing. Marcasites are flat backed while the rhinestones they used were pointed backed, making the hand setting painstaking. They even put this design into gold-tone jewelry, which gave the marcasites a "warm coppery hue" according to Ball and Torem.

Les Bernard designs cover the spectrum of fine tailored-look jewelry, to whimsical figurals, to an Art Deco influence.

Collector/dealer Molly Garza, owner of LeBijouterie et Collage (www.rubylane.com/shops/lebijouterie) told me she loves Les Bernard "because they used imagination in their designs. I like pieces of jewelry that are artistic and speak to me. Les Bernard certainly does that. The quality of workmanship is very good and their pieces are not something you see coming and going." Garza collects Les Bernard necklaces, bracelets and figurals.

Collector/dealer Pat Seal believes Les Bernard jewelry is undervalued by collectors, which is certainly true, as most costume jewelry books either barely mention Les Bernard or don't mention it at all. And since they were in business until the 1990s, many collectors view it as a contemporary manufacturer and overlook it. Seal believes many collectors want big jewelry, and many of the best Les Bernard designs are small.

Now is the time to seek out Les Bernard for your own collection. Many websites and antique stores have Les Bernard jewelry available starting at five or ten dollars, and of course the dealers who know Les Bernard have their most beautiful work priced accordingly. Once collectors realize the quality, genius and talent behind this company, it should become highly sought after and collectible.

Blue flower pin, adjustable petals, opened; these pins came in a 3" style, like this blue one, and a 2½" style, like the red and pink one. The rhinestones inside are a pale blue, the ones on the petals are a medium blue and green. The pins in these colors are real showstoppers, garnering attention whenever they are worn. It took four years to gather the five pins shown here and on the next page, and I only recently found the black one and discovered that they came with matching earrings. All are signed "LES BERNARD INC.," and the stems are all marked "Pat. Pend." The value of the set is $1,000.00. The blue one individually is valued at **$200.00 – 225.00.** All are rare. I have also seen the large size with turquoise-colored rhinestones and in shades of brown. Author collection

Blue flower pin with petals adjusted.

Blue flower pin with petals closed.

Black flower pin with earrings, 3". **$250.00 – 275.00** set. Author collection

Pink and red flower pin, 2½". **$175.00 – 200.00.** Author collection

Gold flower pin, no rhinestones, petals opened, 3". **$75.00 – 95.00.** Author collection

Gold flower pin with rhinestones, 2½". **$125.00 – 150.00.** Author collection

Gold flower pin with rhinestones, back view.

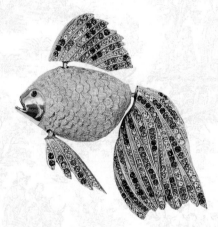

This fish pin in shades of blue is very heavy. All of the fins can move to and fro; this three-dimensional little red-eyed fish is marked "LES BERNARD INC." and "Pat. Pend." As fish pins go, he is a real beauty. Rare. **$225.00 – 250.00.** Author collection

Back of fish pin.

This lion pin features Les Bernard innovations, using flat-back marcasites with pointed-back rhinestones, and using marcasites on a gold-tone metal. Rare. **$150.00 – 175.00.** Author collection

This 3" bow pin has marcasites and blue and green rhinestones. **$95.00 – 115.00.** Author collection

Bow pin and earrings in pink, red, and marcasites. The matching earrings were not the design I would have expected. **$125.00 – 150.00.** Author collection

Circle pin in marcasites and colored cabochons. **$40.00 – 45.00.** Author collection

Large round brooch with dark green cabochon center, with the original tag, 2¼". **$80.00 – 85.00.** Laurel Ladd Ciotti collection

This set has faux opals and blue rhinestones, and its beauty was hard to capture on film. In person, it appears to be real gold and genuine stones. **$100.00 – 125.00.**
Author collection

Close-up of pin.

This little seal pin is less than an inch and a half wide, is gold-washed over sterling, and is marked "STERLING LES BERNARD" in tiny letters across the back. His little tail is tipped with three green rhinestones. **$125.00 – 150.00.**
Author collection

Gold knot earrings that clip on and screw to tighten, marked "Les Bernard." **$25.00 – 30.00.**
Author collection

Little jade bug pendant is similar to a scarab but appears to have legs and eyes. A fun little piece with a Les Bernard Inc. hangtag attached. The back of the bug is also marked "SS." **$40.00 – 50.00.**
Author collection

Strawberry pin, 2" long. **$25.00 –
35.00.** Author collection

Regal set of large, heavy brooch and earrings with lapis and
pearls, all marked. **$50.00 – 65.00.** Author collection

Close-up of pearl in set with lapis; end is dotted
with a tiny clear rhinestone.

Button earrings with clear rhinestones.
$25.00 – 30.00. Author collection

Rhinestone and pearl drop earrings with clip-on back that
screws to tighten; beautiful
design, over 2" long. **$50.00 –
65.00.** Author collection

53

Rhinestone knot necklace, heavy links chain, 16" long with push-in clasp. Marked "LES BERNARD" inside of knot. **$95.00 – 115.00.** Author collection

Heavy gold collar with different shapes and colors of stones. Notice that the back sides extend out to allow collar to be placed around neck. An amazing piece. **$300.00 – 350.00.** Author collection

Black glass beads, individually knotted, with panther head hook with cabochon rhinestone accents to attach to ring; 32" long. **$105.00 – 125.00.** Author collection

Glass lavender beads, each one knotted, with dragon head hook to attach to ring; 22" long. **$80.00 – 95.00.** Author collection

This enormous pin by Les Bernard is marked "THOROBRED WINNERS Created By LES BERNARD TMC." It is 4½" tall and 3⅝" wide. There is a horse head in the center framed by identical horse heads, it is supported by what I believe is a riding crop. I have never seen anything like this before from Les Bernard; it could be some type of award piece. **$75.00 – 95.00.** Author collection

Bogoff

Bogoff is a design firm that has been underappreciated in the past, but has recently begun to come into its own, with collectors actively seeking the lovely designs. The Bogoff Company, which started off as the Spear Novelty Co., dates from 1946 and was headquartered in Chicago, Illinois.

Bogoff jewelry is elegant, with graceful designs using top-quality rhinestones. Most of the jewelry I have personally seen by Bogoff is set in silver-tone metal, mimicking fine jewelry, and I own one bracelet in gold-tone. Necklaces are usually identified at a glance, by the design, which is repeated in a simplified pattern around the back to the clasp. Even the clasps are adorned with rhinestones. The choker style seems to be prevalent also, allowing the beautiful designs to be clearly visible on the wearer.

Bogoff jewelry is not very common, and is snapped up, quickly when available. Recent prices on the Internet have necklaces selling for $75.00 to $125.00, earrings for $25.00 to $50.00 per pair, sets of course going for several hundred dollars, and bracelets, which rarely show up going for as much as $100.00. Bogoff jewelry is very heavy, but actually comfortable to wear, as it was designed to lie gracefully against the wearer's bare skin. There is as much quality craftsmanship in, and on, the back of a piece of Bogoff jewelry as there is on the front.

Bogoff jewelry rivals the best of Eisenberg, Hollycraft and even some Miriam Haskell. The styles are classic and exquisite. Each piece of Bogoff in my collection is clearly marked, even each earring in a pair. I don't believe the company manufactured large quantities of jewelry, as it is uncommon to find. A very few jewelry books show examples, which may be one reason collectors are not more aware of this wonderful designer, but I expect this to change. The best-known designer pieces, such as Schiaparelli, are fast reaching prices far out of the average collector's price range.

Of further note is the son of the original Mr. Bogoff, Steve Bogoff, who can be found in Mill Valley, California, and at info@bogoff.com on the Internet. He is an Antiquarian Horologist (read antique watch collector, restorer and seller.) I have chatted with him via email and he is a very friendly and interesting person. Please let me know if you need further information in contacting Mr. Bogoff.

TIP: One problem I have with necklaces from the 1940s and 1950s is that they were designed to fit much smaller women. My solution is to attach a plain rhinestone bracelet, with a matching style of clasp, and fasten it to the clasp of the necklace, to lengthen the necklace, allowing me to wear them on the outside of my shirt collars.

Clear rhinestone necklace, 16", beautiful mix of round and marquise stones. "Bogoff" is marked under large stone at clasp; hook goes into the rings of the extender. **$75.00 – 100.00.** Author collection.

Clear rhinestone flower choker, 14½" long, signed under the flower with the push in clasp, heavy construction, beautifully handcrafted. **$125.00 – 150.00.** Author collection

Bogoff

Necklace with mark.

Bright topaz yellow stone bracelet with safety chain, 7". Most Bogoff jewelry is in silver-tone metal; this gold-tone piece is rare. **$150.00 – 175.00.** Author collection

Two pair of earrings that can be worn with the necklace below left; earrings are screw on and are marked on the flat back of the screw. **$30.00 – 40.00** per pair. Author collection

Pale peridot choker, with two shades of stones, 14". Bogoff's colored jewelry is gorgeous and well made. **$150.00 – 175.00.** Author collection

View of back of necklaces and bracelet; note the unique construction of the links.

Hobé

Recently I bought a Hobé bracelet via mail, sight unseen, with only a vague description. Many people might be shocked at that. Costume jewelry collectors not only understand, but approve, and might even be a little jealous.

Hobé (pronounced hoe-bay) jewelry is one of the best designed and manufactured jewelry available, today and for more than one hundred years. The first Hobé designer and manufacturer was Jacques Hobé, a well-known jeweler in Paris in the late 1880s. His designs were primarily fine jewelry, but he developed one revolutionary concept: make quality jewelry affordable to people besides the wealthy society. The Industrial Revolution was in its infancy, and manufacturing processes were making mass production a viable concept.

Jacques decided he could make jewelry in metals other than gold and silver, and use stones other than diamonds and precious stones. The one thing he decided not to substitute was the handcrafting each piece would receive. The most important things were maintaining quality in design and manufacture. His successful innovations were carried to America by his son William.

America warmly embraced William, from New York to Hollywood. His unique creations were so sought after by Hollywood stars that Hobé opened a shop at 311 North Beverly Drive. Hobé designed not only jewelry but costume designs for the stars as well. Beginning in the 1940s, the most popular movie stars promoted the Hobé line, whose slogan was "Jewels of Legendary Splendor."

And splendid they still are, luxurious even, with their antique flair, the brilliant designs using the very best quality of rhinestones, the intricate twisting and weaving done in fine wire and the special detailing such as careful soldering that remains hidden.

Jacques's innovation and imagination continue be to passed down through each generation of Hobé. William's sons Robert and David were also designers, using unique stones and beads sought worldwide, and they hold the exclusive rights to the high quality imitation pearls from the Spanish Island of Majorca.

Do you remember in the 1980s when the pearl enhancer first appeared? We owe that innovation to Jim Hobé, son of Robert. One of their most recent additions to the Hobé line is the cleverly designed clasp that turns the two strand pearl necklace into a long single strand of pearls.

The Hobé trademarks throughout the years reflect their superior quality and reputation.

The marks are as follows:
A fleur-de-lis with "Hobé" on it, used before 1868.
A crown with "Hobé" inside, used during 1868.
Crossed swords over the word *Hobé*, from 1883 – 1902.
"Hobé" in a rounded emerald shape, from 1903 – 1917.
"Hobé Design Pat." inside a squared-off triangle, from 1918 – 1932.
"Hobé Design Pat." inside a triangle, from 1933 – 1957.
"Hobé" inside an oval, beginning in 1958.
Other marks included "Hobé" inside a rectangle and "Hobé Sterling Pat. Pend.," along with the paper tags of "Jewels of Legendary Splendor Hobé."

Oh, did I forget to tell you the rest of the Hobé bracelet story? First, it was described as: "Hobé bracelet, rhinestone clasp, crystal beads on silver chain with fat pearls." I had a check for my birthday for $30.00; the price including shipping for the Hobé was $30.00. It was fate.

The day the box arrived, I sat down in the living room and carefully opened it. Truthfully, I had no idea what it might look like, or what condition it might be in. I slowly unwrapped the tissue paper, revealing a bracelet so breathtaking I was glad I was sitting down. I actually had to set the bracelet down on the arm of the chair, so I could just look at it for a few minutes. The rhinestone clasp is huge, a pair of attached pavéd domes, with beautiful crystal beads strung on a delicate silver chain, separated by large oval pearls with rhinestone rondelles on either side. It is the most comfortable bracelet I own, and I receive compliments from complete strangers every time I wear it. Thank you, Hobé family.

Gilt leaf necklace, 16", with pearls and aurora borealis rivoli beads, book chain. Has matching bracelet and earrings. Only the earrings are signed. **$175.00 – 225.00** parure.
Kim Paff collection

Gilt leaf bracelet of same set.

Gilt leaf earrings of same set.

Four-strand necklace, signed, all glass, black and red beads, crystal rondelles and pearls, strung on chain, note dangle at clasp. **$300.00 – 325.00** set.
Kim Paff collection

Matching bracelet; note elaborate clasp on wire wrap bracelet, which is not signed but clearly a perfect match. Kim Paff collection

Matching signed earrings.

Smoky glass beads and plastic white faceted beads, 18" necklace. **$150.00 – 165.00** set.
Kim Paff collection

Wire-wrapped bracelet to match, with dangles at back.

Matching earrings, signed.

Three-strand black faceted beads with pearls and crystal rondelles, 16" – 21" strands, has matching earrings, **$125.00 – 135.00** set.
Kim Paff collection

Matching earrings, signed.

Single strand necklace with red aurora borealis and black beads and rondelles, not signed but matching the earrings. **$75.00 – 95.00** set. Kim Paff collection

Matching earrings, signed.

Smoky faceted crystal beads with red plastic glitter beads and crystal rondelles. Strands are from 16" to 20". **$95.00 – 110.00.** Kim Paff collection

Two-strand necklace and matching earrings, in center of photo; sectagonal beads are plastic with gold filigree, smoky beads are glass; 20" long. **$150.00 – 165.00** set. Kim Paff collection

White and peridot glass two-strand necklace, 18" – 20", with matching earrings, all signed. **$150.00 – 165.00.** Kim Paff collection

Carded sets of Hobé earrings, **$25.00 – 30.00** per pair. All Kim Paff collection

Blues.

Pinks.

Pale pinks with pearls.

Dark button.

White flower.

Black beads.

Elaborate pink wrap bracelet, with plastic beads and crystal rondelles, has trademark elaborate dangles on bracelet ends. Unsigned. **$170.00 – 180.00.** Kim Paff collection

Green and black two strand necklace with black aurora borealis beads, green rondelles, green aurora borealis rivoli beads and matching signed dangling earrings. Strands are 16" and 18". Notice the earrings have a square bead identical to the ones on the necklace set into a round prong setting at the top of the earring. **$175.00 – 185.00** set.

Kim Paff collection

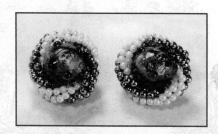

Golden topaz and pearl flapper necklace, in Hobé style, matches wrap bracelet and earrings. **$240.00 – 260.00.**

Kim Paff collection

Golden topaz and pearl wrap bracelet, unsigned.

Golden topaz and pearl earrings, signed.

Blue chunky "Wilma" beads wrap bracelet and matching earrings, blue plastic beads, mother-of-pearl and gold-tone beads. **$75.00 – 85.00** set.
Kim Paff collection

Wrap bracelet in clear plastic and glass aurora borealis beads, with signed matching earrings. **$85.00 – 95.00.**
Kim Paff collection

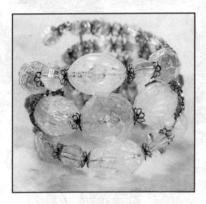

Close-up of front of bracelet.

Two-strand necklace, black plastic beads, pearls, crystal beads, and rondelles; matching bracelet with large gold filigree balls and dangles, matching signed earrings. **$225.00 – 230.00.** Kim Paff collection

Two-strand signed necklace with wrap bracelet, red and pink chunky plastic beads, and plastic silver filigree. **$45.00 – 65.00.**
Kim Paff collection

Two-strand topaz aurora borealis necklace and unsigned wrap bracelet; all glass beads, 16" and 18" long. **$120.00 – 135.00.** Kim Paff collection

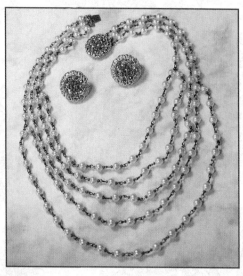

Pearl and coral bead necklace and earrings, three strands becoming five strands, earrings only are signed. **$95.00 – 110.00.** Kim Paff collection

Cobalt blue glass beads and pearls unsigned wrap bracelet and earrings in the same style. **$100.00 – 110.00.** Kim Paff collection

Orange aurora borealis glass bead wrap bracelet and earrings in the same style. **$100.00 – 110.00.** Kim Paff collection

Unsigned Hobé-style set of necklace and earrings with pearls and black plastic beads. **$30.00 – 45.00.** Kim Paff collection

Gold-tone mesh dangles pin. **$65.00 – 75.00.**
Nancy Canãs collection

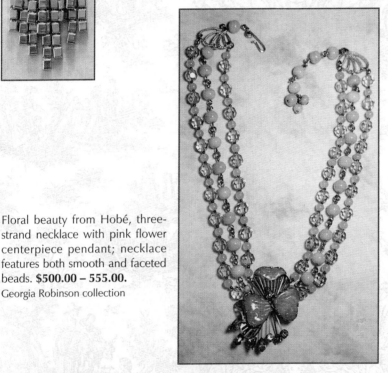

Floral beauty from Hobé, three-strand necklace with pink flower centerpiece pendant; necklace features both smooth and faceted beads. **$500.00 – 555.00.**
Georgia Robinson collection

Fun strawberry necklace, unusual offering from Hobé. **$200.00 – 225.00.** Nancy Canãs collection

This set of necklace and bracelet features green, blue, and lavender rhinestones; the necklace is 17" long, in gold-tone metal. **$600.00 – 650.00.**
Georgia Robinson collection

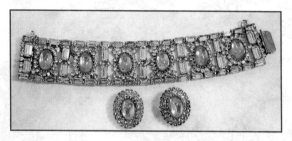

Demi parure of rhinestones and faux opals. **$175.00 – 225.00.** Nancy Canãs collection

This parure features deep amethyst rhinestones and pale lavender stones; it is an amazing find in unworn condition. **$700.00 – 750.00.** Nancy Canãs collection

Black art glass and Coralene red beads feature prominently on this all-plastic-bead necklace and earring set. Necklace is strung on trademark Hobé chain. **$95.00 – 120.00.** Author collection

Note: Coralene was a patented process in which tiny glass balls were fused to larger beads. Information courtesy of Eclecticala.com

Pale lavender plastic beads are accented with flower petal bead caps that Hobé used in many ways make up this demi-parure, 18" necklace; two-strand bracelet extends to 8". **$150.00 – 165.00.** Author collection

Wrap bracelet in pink, white, and green, with leaves; pink and green beads are glass, moonstone beads are plastic, elaborate dangles on both ends of bracelet. A priceless gift from a dear friend. Priced anyway, **$200.00 – 210.00.** Author collection

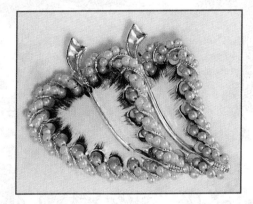

Enameled leaves wrapped in pearls pin; pearl wrap goes through holes in leaves and wraps around back. **$100.00 – 125.00.** Author collection

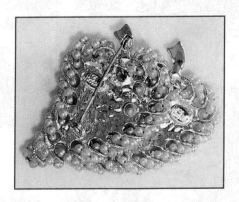

Pearl leaves pin back view.

Black glass bead medallion necklace. **$100.00 – 120.00.** Author collection

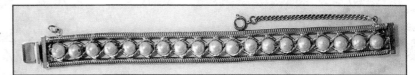

Mesh bracelet with pearls and safety chain. **$35.00 – 40.00.** Author collection

My personal favorite Hobé demi-parure, with pearls and rhinestones. So many pieces of jewelry do not photograph well but are stunning in person; this set is one of those. The pearls are plastic and the crystals are glass, strung on chain; the bracelet has a large pavéd rhinestone clasp. **$250.00 – 300.00** set, but I wouldn't sell it for $500.00. Author collection

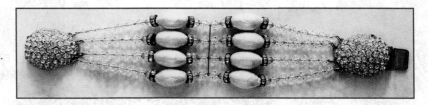

Close-up view of bracelet.

Completely different bangle bracelet with colored cabochons. **$150.00 – 165.00.** Kim Paff collection

Volupté

When most people hear the name Volupté, they immediately think of compacts. Or cigarette cases. Or lighters. Or carryalls, atomizers or pillboxes. Few people will think of costume jewelry. But for a very limited time, Volupté made top-quality costume jewelry. Because of this brief period, Volupté jewelry is scarce.

The company was started in 1926, and produced fine ladies' accessories until the late 1950s or early 1960s. It had the fashionable address of 347 Fifth Avenue, New York City.

Kathy Burch, owner of Tri-State Antique Center in Canonsburg, Pennsylvania, has been collecting, buying and selling compacts for over twenty years. Burch states that "Volupté was always creative and aggressive in their advertising, they even hosted a radio quiz show once a week called *The Better Half*. Always with an eye to the future, Volupté was ahead of their time in the late forties when they marketed their Collector's Items line. The company hired such movie stars as Rita Hayworth and Dorothy Lamour to appear in advertisements claiming that 'Hollywood stars collected them.' It proved to be a prophetic line, as today these items are highly collectible and much in demand to compact collectors."

A full page ad from *Harper's Bazaar*, 1948, has Rita Hayworth stating "collecting compacts like these is an exciting idea." The compacts sold for five to fifteen dollars. The ad also states that Volupté would send at no charge an illustrated booklet called *"Collector's Items* by Volupté . . . unusual, fascinating hints on decorating your home with compacts." My favorite part of the ad, besides the fact that it features my favorite glamour star Rita Hayworth, is the tag line of "Volupté reflects the prettiest faces." How's that for making a woman feel special?

Burch said that "Volupté jewelry was of the finest quality and quite beautiful, but extremely rare to find today as the company focused largely on compact production." Volupté jewelry may be completely unknown to most jewelry collectors because it is rarely seen in jewelry books. Joanne Dubbs Ball shows one necklace with matching earrings in her book *Costume Jewelers, The Golden Age of Design*. Ball values the set at $350.00 to $450.00. She states that "their jewelry was of very fine quality and also quite beautiful. It is rarely seen today."

Cherri Simonds agrees in her book *Collectible Costume Jewelry,* saying "jewelry by this company is rare." Simonds shows a one-half-inch wide chromium-plated mesh choker valued at $120.00 to $180.00. After two years of actively searching for Volupté I have only managed to find one set of necklace and earrings, one single pair of earrings, two necklaces and two bracelets.

Each month when I decide what I will feature in my next column, I immerse myself in all the information I can find; I have to tell you, Volupté has not only been educational, it has been fun. I contacted Kathy Burch after seeing the compacts featured on her website, found at www.tri-stateantiques.com. I had never seen such beautiful compacts, truly small works of art. And the prices were also amazing, up to almost two thousand dollars. Not all her compacts are priced that high; they start around one hundred thirty-five dollars and go up. Her website itself is a work of art, one of the quickest at downloading I have seen, with clear photographs and descriptions of the items she offers, which include everything you would find in a high-quality antique center.

This is one of the best examples of Volupté jewelry; it has style, crafts-manship, a beautiful design, and excellent stone selection in color and shape. Both screw-on earrings are marked, and the 16" necklace has a hangtag. The design of the necklace lies to the side, instead of straight down. I have seen this exact design with these blue stones, ruby red, and all clears. **$150.00 – 185.00.** Author collection

Pendant features almost all the standard shapes of clear rhinestones; 15½" long, with a hang tag at the hook. **$120.00 – 135.00.** Author collection

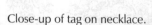

Close-up of tag on necklace.

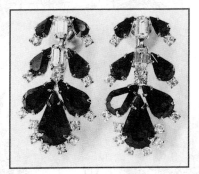

Red earrings in the same design as the blue set. **$40.00 – 45.00.** Author collection

This hand-knotted pearl bracelet feels and shows like the real thing; it has a push-in clasp that disappears into the rhinestone sphere. The end of the sphere is marked in tiny, nearly invisible letters. **$75.00 – 85.00.** Author collection

Leaf motif bracelet, 7" long. **$30.00 – 40.00.** Author collection

Baguette necklace with clear stones, 14" long, name plate is soldered onto back of last two baguette links in necklace. **$100.00 – 125.00.** Author collection

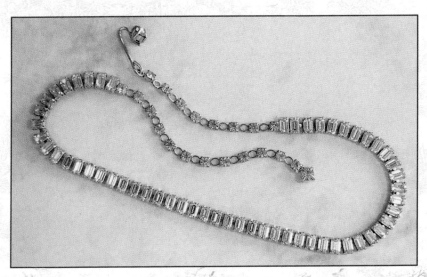

Quality

Why can you pick up a little rhinestone pin and the price is less than $10.00, while another that looks similar may be priced at $100.00? Why were these pieces priced differently when they were first available for sale? The answers may be superior design and workmanship qualities. A closer look, often under magnification, will reveal the handwork involved in many of the older pieces of costume jewelry.

I recently had to rebuild a Miriam Haskell brooch of a simple design, with tiny pearls surrounding a clover pattern. First the pin had to be separated, back from front, which had been wired on. Next the wired-on pearls had to be removed, and the dead rhinestones replaced. Each section, eighteen total, of the design had 11 strands of five pearls each, with the beading wire flat underneath the top half. What had appeared to be a simple job required almost 10 hours of work to reattach. Each strand needed the tiny pearls strung, then wrapped around the base, then wrapped again to secure them in place, before moving on to the next strand. Though perfectly beautiful when completed, it made me realize that there is more to making a vintage costume jewelry purchase than in simply liking the looks of that piece.

Brenda Sue Lansdowne of B'Sue Boutiques in East Palestine, Ohio, is an award-winning jewelry designer, in addition to collecting and selling costume jewelry. She states, "the fact is, in quality collectible jewelry OR new high-end lines, what you have is the jeweler's art. No matter that it happens to be worked in something less than 14kt. gold, principles are the same. Or perhaps even more painstaking because the metals may not be as durable, in some cases, or because there is plating involved. Still the designs are many times worked out on paper just as an architect would design a building, and prototypes cast in sterling first. It is precision all the way."

"Haskell jewelry was an art," Lansdown continues. "It's not just something you sit down and do. Take repairing a brooch. The tension on the wire has to be just right, and the beads have to fit properly. The finishing work is critical, or the wire strands will break. If the tension is wrong, or the beads the wrong size, you will not have a work of art. You will have a blob."

Rhinestone jewelry in particular can have a great deal of handwork. When the stones in a pavéd piece were set, artisans could not merely sweep a large brush stroke of glue over the entire surface and throw stones on top. Glue must be gently placed in each space, then each stone, one at a time, set into the mounting. If these stones are prong set, that means a minimum of four prongs per stone. Austrian jewelry many times has elaborate prong settings, with as many as 16 prongs. Imagine the price of a piece of jewelry today if someone had to sit for three or four hours setting stones into just one necklace.

Fellow repairwoman Carol Johnston agrees. "Hand-set stones are a challenge. Quite often the owner will bend the prongs into the cup when they lose a stone so that they won't be catching the piece on anything. When stones pop out of a prong set piece it is usually because the cup has become skewed during wear. When I get the piece, I then find it necessary to lift the prongs back out of the cup and sometimes reshape the cup. This can be a real challenge."

Patricia Youngblood of The Antiques and Collectibles Store of Plymouth, Pennsylvania, knows it takes a discriminating eye to quickly detect superior design, workmanship and quality. "Nearly invariably, the finer costume pieces reflect the work of renowned designers and superb artisans; therefore, people who have such discriminating taste and the financial ability to do so, usually are willing to pay more for the designer pieces."

Sometimes a designer mark seems to automatically add to the value of jewelry. Upon closer examination into the handwork and workmanship of each piece, the value will seem more realistic. Many designers required top-quality production of their jewelry before they would allow their name to be placed on it. These designers had a specific idea in mind, from the drawing board to completion, and didn't care what was involved in producing the jewelry, as long as it came out beautifully constructed. There are many designers today still making costume jewelry with rhinestones, but rarely will you find it featuring prong set stones, most are glued.

Quality

And many collectors of jewelry today totally ignore costume, preferring fine jewelry. Costume collectors know that the jewelry they are so passionate about is every bit as wonderful as fine jewelry, and the workmanship of so much that is still available is of top quality. As Brenda Sue Lansdowne declares, "Before anyone poo-poos costume, they need to take a deep breath and examine the artistry involved. It's not just anyone who can design and execute a viable piece of costume jewelry, and it's not just anyone who can fix it if it breaks. It takes talent, skill, and an eye for form, flow and movement. Oh, and the patience of a saint!"

I went to the Jewelcollect club to find out how these collectors wear their dress clips. I got answers from Pam Wiggins of Depression Delights, Susan in Boston, Massachusetts, and Joan Vogel Elias. Joan says dress clips look gorgeous on boots, purses, belts, pockets, jacket lapels, shoes, sleeves and hats. Susan says she prefers to wear dress clips to brooches, and wears them in her hair by clipping them to safety pins and attaching them to the hair ornament. She also uses safety pins to attach them to chains to wear as pendants. Pam Wiggins compiled a list of ten ways to wear dress clips. They include: 1) Hang a small one on a chain as a slide-type pendant. 2) Pin a safety pin on the inside of a blouse or sweater and "hang" a clip on it. 3) Wear one as a barrette in your hair. 4) Use as a scarf clip. 5) Tuck into the pocket on a pair of jeans. 6) Clip into the "V" of a V-necked dress or blouse. 7) Clip a pair into the bottom corners of a square neckline. 8) Clip one onto the round neck of a sweater. 9) Clip at the neck of a tailored blouse in place of a tie. 10) Use a pair on your pumps, as shoe ornaments, for a day to evening look. Thanks everyone!

This Réja flower fur clip has seen better days, but that only shows that it was well loved. Or maybe thrown in a jewelry box carelessly! It has substantial weight for the size, and each pistil has its own little red or clear rhinestone. The enameling is quite dinged, but I have decided not to restore it. 3½" x 2½", nearly 1" thick. **$300.00 – 350.00.** Author collection

This dragon brooch is a classic example of marcasite and rhinestone jewelry. The details of the dragon's face and talons are exquisite. The brooch is not marked, but appears to be sterling. This type of attention to detail is rarely seen in contemporary jewelry. **$200.00 – 250.00.** Author collection

Back view of dragon marcasite pin.

Lucite Trifari Moonshell pin/fur clip and matching earrings with the Crown Trifari mark. **$550.00 – 600.00.** Author collection

This bar pin is European, according to the trombone clasp. The rhinestone quality makes it appear as if this were genuine gemstones and diamonds. It is 2⅝" long. **$100.00 – 125.00.** Author collection

Back view of bar pin.

This Original by Robert pin garners attention each time it is worn, from people asking if it is a popular peanut butter and chocolate candy pin. The large stones are completely enclosed in the back. The back of this pin is just as beautiful as the front. **$150.00 – 200.00.** Author collection

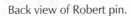

Back view of Robert pin.

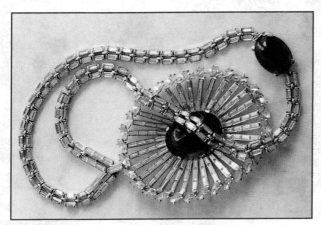

Trifari necklace, clear rhinestone chain, ruby center and clasp stones, 15" long, center is 3" long. **$155.00 – 175.00.** Patti Collins Bultman collection

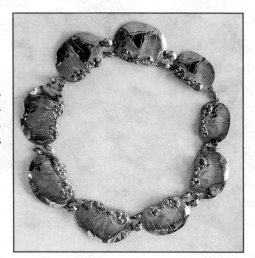

This sterling hand-wrought lily pad choker was made by Mary Gage. There was limited production of this style, and it was found only in the Northeast. **$1,500.** Kim Paff collection

Close-up of Mary Gage signature.

This pearl enhancer is signed "Rifas," and has summer white hand-wired beads and matching earrings. The gold filigree enhancer is 1¼". **$100.00 – 115.00.** Kim Paff collection

Back view of Rifas enhancer.

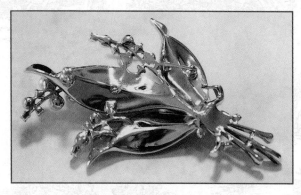

Back view of Trifari brooch.

Crown Trifari lily of the valley demi-parure, with faux pearls, clear rhinestones, and enameled leaves. **$400.00 – 600.00.** Nancy Canãs collection

Boucher 2820 Art Deco brooch with
clear rhinestones. **$95.00 – 130.00.**
Nancy Canās collection

Back view of brooch.

Butler & Wilson twin Scotties pin,
enameled with clear rhinestone
eyes and collars. **$75.00 – 95.00.**
Nancy Canās collection

Back view of Scottie pin.

Trifari gold-tone fur clip, almost 4" long,
blue enamel with pearls and rhinestones, floral spray. **$350.00 – 425.00.**
Georgia Robinson collection

Ledo cuff bracelet with shades of topaz and honey gold champagne rhinestones; cuff has safety chain. The design and workmanship on the back of the bracelet are beautiful. **$95.00 – 115.00.** Georgia Robinson collection

Back view of bracelet.

Close-up of mark on bracelet.

Vendôme starburst pin, light and dark amber and green rhinestones; many of the stones are mounted upside down, 2½" diameter. **$85.00 – 105.00.** Patti Collins Bultman collection

Reverse view of Vendôme pin.

Pair of Robert Mandle rhinestone birds in flight with red eyes; wing tip to wing tip is 2½", they are almost 2" tall, and both are marked. **$175.00 – 200.00** pair. Patti Collins Bultman collection

Close-up of bird pin.

Robert Mandle dragonfly, 2" x 1½", clear rhinestones, not marked but a personal gift to owner from Mandle. **$175.00 – 190.00.** Patti Collins Bultman collection

Robert Mandle necklace, black and amber, 26" long, octagon beads are two-toned, black inside. One of a kind, a personal gift to owner. **$250.00 – 265.00.** Patti Collins Bultman collection

Original by Robert dangle pin with pearls, marquise rhine-stones, clear beads, almost 4" long. **$100.00 – 125.00.**
Patti Collins Bultman collection

Mother-of-pearl bracelet, square links with pearls and colored rhinestone accents, large fold-over clasp, 7" long, attributed to Jonné. **$300.00 – 325.00.** Patti Collins Bultman collection

Schiaparelli parure, watermelon stones, only pin is signed. **$250.00 – 300.00.** Nancy Canãs collection

Close-up view of Schiaparelli pin.

Back view of Schiaparelli.

Trifari sterling vermeil bird of paradise; this design came in a variety of stone combinations, all stones are unfoiled, and piece is 3" long. Slightly illegible numbers read "#142659." Featured in a 1945 ad. **$350.00 – 400.00.** Georgia Robinson collection

Reverse view of Trifari bird pin.

Miriam Haskell six-strand coral bead bracelet with genuine shell clasp, a variety of stones, and seed pearl accents. **$550.000 – 600.00.** Georgia Robinson collection

Back view of Haskell bracelet.

Eisenberg Original green brooch, 4" long; the tiny rhinestones were painted at one time, and the large center glass cabochon is simulated malachite and is 1½" long. **$650.00 – 700.00.** Georgia Robinson collection

Back view of Eisenberg Original brooch.

Ciro fur clip, absolutely stunning, looks like fine jewelry, very high-quality clear and emerald rhinestones, in never worn condition; note clear rhinestone baguettes curling over top of design; fur clip is 1½" wide. **$250.00 – 275.00.** Author collection

Back view of Ciro fur clip.

Ciro fur clip with matching earrings, green rhinestones; clip is 1½", earrings are 1" clip on. Never worn condition. **$150.00 – 175.00.** Author collection

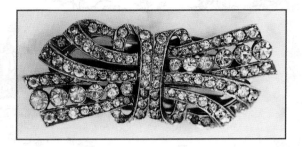

Close-up of pin.

Ciro of Bond St. London & New York duette in clear rhinestones in original box. **$80.00 – 95.00.** Author collection

Lily Daché clear rhinestone clip, fabric locks into back of clip, 1½" wide. Rare. **$125.00 – 140.00.** Author collection

Lily Daché clear rhinestone necklace, 14½", flower pendant with large rhinestones, signed on back of pendant. Rare. **$300.00 – 350.00.** Author collection

Lily Daché flower pin, two shades of yellow, clear and green rhinestones. Flower is attached to stem in such a way as to allow pin movement when worn. Rare. **$350.00 – 400.00.**
Author collection

Trifari swirl fur clips with clear stones, 1¾" long, Trifanium. **$245.00 – 255.00** pair.
Laurel Ladd Ciotti collection

Coro prancing donkey pin with blue eye and large red marquise stone ears. Originally came with matching earrings. **$200.00 – 250.00.**
Laurel Ladd Ciotti collection

Réja gazelle, gold wash, with clear rhinestones, 3¾" tall. **$195.00 – 210.00.**
Laurel Ladd Ciotti collection

Eisenberg Original fur clip, Josephine Baker, large pink stones. This pin was also made by Reinad and Chanel Novelty — same pin, different signatures. **$1,200.00 – 1,500.00.**
Laurel Ladd Ciotti collection

Weiss shades of blue and green cabochons bracelet and brooch, large stones, rhodium plated. **$185.00 – 205.00.** Nancy Canãs collection

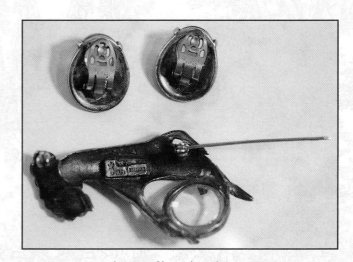

Trifari Crown Sterling jelly belly demi-parure, hand brooch and clip earrings, jelly belly, gold wash with clear rhinestones. **$1,300.00 – 2,000.00.** Nancy Canãs collection

Back view of brooch and earrings.

Hamilton & Hamilton, Jr. (in business in Providence, Rhode Island, from 1883 – 1922), sterling glove clips. Rare. **$145.00 – 155.00.** Laurel Ladd Ciotti collection

Silver-tone hand-figural glove holder, with aqua rhinestones, 2" long. **$50.00 – 85.00.** Kim Paff collection

Eisenberg necklace in original box, green and clear rhinestones, 16" necklace. **$125.00 – 150.00.** Author collection

Close-up of necklace.

Chanel diamonté bow pin features a large faux pearl drop, 2¾" tall. **$595.00 – 655.00.** Treasures-in-Time collection

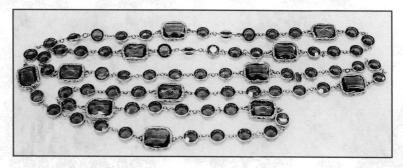

Chanel gold-plated bangle with red and green Gripoix cabochons, signed in a plaque "Chanel, Made in France," the double C mark, and the numbers *2* and *3*; 2¾" across and 7½" around the inside. **$595.00 – 655.00.** Treasures-in-Time collection

Chanel amethyst crystal necklace from 1981, features round and rectangle crystals in a gold-plated setting; if you look closely at the chain, on the right-hand side three rows from the top, you will see the signed hang tag between two round crystals. **$495.00 – 550.00.** Treasures-in-Time collection

Adorable mama and baby elephant scatter pins with clear rhinestones and red rhinestone eyes, signed "Chanel," in script. This mark is believed to be the mark of the Chanel Novelty Company, not related to the company owned by Coco Chanel. Both elephants are signed. **$295.00 – 325.00.** Treasures-in-Time collection

Chanel pin/pendant with blue Gripoix glass stones and faux pearls; glass is cobalt blue, pale blue, and aqua; gold-tone, 3" across. **$765.00 – 810.00.** Treasures-in-Time collection

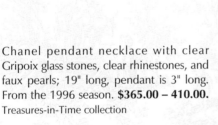

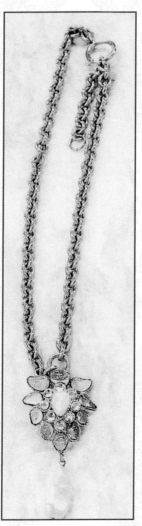

Chanel pendant necklace with clear Gripoix glass stones, clear rhinestones, and faux pearls; 19" long, pendant is 3" long. From the 1996 season. **$365.00 – 410.00.** Treasures-in-Time collection

Chanel gold-tone pin with red and green Gripoix glass stones and faux pearls, 2". **$325.00 – 345.00.** Treasures-in-Time collection

Chanel gold-plated pin with molded glass and metal scarabs, 3" x 2½", signed on oval on back: "Chanel, Made in France," with the double C logo and the numbers *2* and *8*. **$445.00 – 475.00.** Treasures-in-Time collection

McClelland Barclay gold-tone bracelet with three large emerald-cut, green, open-back rhinestones accented with clear and green smaller rhinestones, 7" long and ¾" wide. **$175.00 – 200.00.** Treasures-in-Time collection

Rifas Art Deco pin and earrings with rectangular and square emerald green glass stones accented with clear and black stones, with a marbled dangling glass drop; the square green stones are set with stripes of marcasites, the pin is 3" long, the earrings are 2". **$375.00 – 400.** Treasures-in-Time collection

Earrings.

DeMario baroque pearl bracelet with fancy clasp of pearls and rhinestones, 7" long. **$135.00 – 165.00.** Treasures-in-Time collection

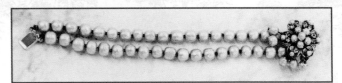

DeMario necklace of pale pink beads and rhinestone rondelles, centerpiece has striped red, and white seed beads with pink, red, and lavender rhinestones, and pink and yellow enameled leaves; signed on clasp. **$200.00 – 225.00.** Treasures-in-Time collection

DeMario pin with iridescent cream seed beads wired to a gold gilt setting, cream and beige beads dangle at the bottom, accented with an amber rhinestone flower, 2½". **$115.00 – 135.00.**
Treasures-in-Time collection

DeMario brooch of pink crystal and aurora borealis rhinestones in a gold-tone setting, 2⅜" tall. **$65.00 – 75.00.**
Treasures-in-Time collection

DeMario pin with seed pearls, rhinestones, and baroque pearls, accented throughout with gold-tone leaves, signed "Robert DeMario NYC," 1¾" wide. **$125.00 – 145.00.**
Treasures-in-Time collection

Eisenberg fur clip with clear rhinestones, 1¼" x 1⅛", signed with a script *E*. **$185.00 – 225.00.**
Treasures-in-Time collection

Eisenberg Original fur clip with emerald green stones, 4" x 2¾", signed "Eisenberg Original" and the number 5 in a circle; clip is constructed of several molded sections. **$300.00 – 350.00.** Treasures-in-Time collection

Unsigned but attributed to Eisenberg pin in aqua and clear faceted rhinestones set in silver-tone setting. Most of the stones are open backed and unfoiled, 3¼" tall and 2" wide; the large clear oval stone is 1½" x 1". **$325.00 – 400.00.** Treasures-in-Time collection

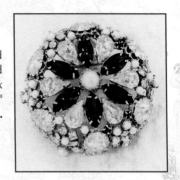

Schreiner New York domed pin/pendant with clear and amethyst stones and faux pearls, 2½" wide, nearly 1" deep. **$360.00 – 395.00.** Treasures-in-Time collection

Schreiner smoky aurora borealis rhinestone pin and earrings set in gunmetal; pin is 3" wide, earrings are 1½ " tall, signed "Schreiner." **$225.00 – 250.00.** Treasures-in-Time collection

Schreiner New York smoky topaz, golden topaz, and clear rhinestone pin and earrings set; pin is 2¼" square, earrings are 1" tall; one earring and the pin are signed. **$375.00 – 425.00.** Treasures-in-Time collection

Vibrant orange Schreiner New York mosaic pin/pendant features four large orange and white mosaic plaques measuring 1¼" x ⅞"; pin measures 3" across and has two hooks to allow it to be used as a pendant. **$450.00 – 500.00.** Treasures-in-Time collection

Schreiner set in smoky and clear rhinestones, round snowflake design. **$175.00 – 200.00.** Treasures-in-Time collection

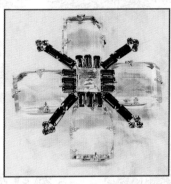 

Schreiner set in clear, smoke and amber rhinestones, pin/pendant and earrings, the large clear rhinestones are 1¼" x 1", one earring and the pin are signed "Schreiner New York." **$600.00 – 650.00.** Treasures-in-Time collection

Miriam Haskell green and blue glass bib necklace with faux pearls, 15" long, dangles hang 1½ ", signed on the back of the clasp. **$525.00 – 575.00.** Treasures-in-Time collection

Miriam Haskell blue and green glass pin with faux pearls, silver-tone with a gunmetal finish, 2⅜". **$225.00 – 260.00.** Treasures-in-Time collection

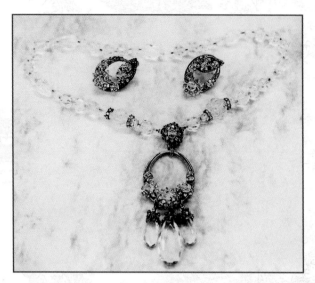

Miriam Haskell demi-parure of crystal and Lucite, necklace and earrings; the necklace clasp is in the front and suspends the pendant. The necklace is 18" long, with a 3⅓" long pendant; earrings are 1⅜", all pieces are signed. **$450.00 – 500.00.** Treasures-in-Time collection

Miriam Haskell black rhinestone pin, 2⅝" diameter and 1¼ " deep. **$350.00 – 375.00.** Treasures-in-Time collection

Miriam Haskell horseshoe signature 1940s faux pearl pin with faux seed pearls and rose montees, 2". **$175.00 – 195.00.** Treasures-in-Time collection

Miriam Haskell gilt metal necklace and earrings set with marbled green plastic cabochon, designed by Larry Vrba in 1973; necklace is adjustable from 13" to 16", earrings are 1½", all pieces are signed. **$300.00 – 350.00.** Treasures-in-Time collection

Miriam Haskell three-strand chain bracelet with large and small faux baroque pearls; slide-in clasp, over 7" long, signed on back of clasp. **$100.00 – 125.00.** Treasures-in-Time collection

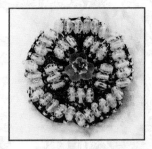

Miriam Haskell pink glass hinged bangle bracelet; has beads wired together on a pierced gold-plated brass frame, signed on an oval disk in the inside of the bracelet, ¾" wide. **$325.00 – 365.00.** Treasures-in-Time collection

Miriam Haskell blue glass bead pin, with wired-on beads in a flower shape, signed on horseshoe plaque on the back, 2". **$125.00 – 145.00.** Treasures-in-Time collection

Miriam Haskell bracelet with gold-tone flowers with pearl centers, flowing gold-tone scrollwork and dangling faux baroque pearls, 7½" long, ⅝" wide, with a safety chain. **$300.00 – 350.00.** Treasures-in-Time collection

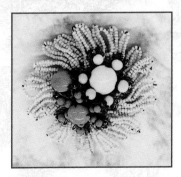

Miriam Haskell baroque pearl necklace with rose montees and rhinestone rondelles, 22" long with a 2½" drop; safety closure on the necklace bears the patent number 3427691, beginning date of 1969. **$375.00 – 400.00.** Treasures-in-Time collection

Miriam Haskell white seed bead pin with white and coral glass bead and cabochon center, 2¾" wide, signed on back. **$135.00 – 155.00.** Treasures-in-Time collection

Miriam Haskell hinged bangle bracelet, gold-tone brass filigree with twisted rope border settings for two shades of glass coral beads, safety chain; bracelet is 6¾" x ½", signed on an oval plaque on the inside near the clasp. **$140.00 – 160.00.** Treasures-in-Time collection

Miriam Haskell glass agate pin, prong-set agate with wired-on glass beads, 2¼", signed "Miriam Haskell." **$215.00 – 245.00.** Treasures-in-Time collection

Miriam Haskell gilt metal necklace with dangling faceted black beads, graduated from center to back, 15" long, signed on oval hang tag, also has patent number 3427691 on the clasp dating to the mid 1960s. **$250.00 – 300.00.** Treasures-in-Time collection

Miriam Haskell pin designed in gilt metal with a large baby blue molded glass center stone and small glass beads in yellow and blue, all beads wired on, 2". **$190.00 – 220.00.** Treasures-in-Time collection

Miriam Haskell coral bead pin with coral cabochon center in a gold-tone setting, 2" wide. **$260.00 – 295.00.** Treasures-in-Time collection

Early unsigned Miriam Haskell cornflower blue bracelet with matching clip, all glass beads and glass leaf shapes, bracelet is 7" long, clip is 2¾" wide. **$475.00 – 525.00.** Treasures-in-Time collection

Unsigned Miriam Haskell clip, painted wood beads and silk-wrapped metal heart designed by Frank Hess ca. 1925 – 1930; a bright and happy clip. **$155.00 – 175.00.** Treasures-in-Time collection

Jeanne pin in marbled yellow and faux lapis cabochons, unfoiled stones set in an open-back gold-plated setting, 2" wide. **$100.00 – 135.00**. Treasures-in-Time collection

K.J.L. bib necklace with flat cobalt rectangular bezel-set rhinestones, clear stones, and coral glass dangles, gold plated, 16" long and 3" at center. **$1,525.00 – 1,625.00.** Treasures-in-Time collection

K.J.L. goony bird has a swivel belly so that you can have two different looks, 2⅜" x 2", rhinestones and enamel. Both sides of belly shown. **$300.00 – 325.00.** Treasures-in-Time collection

Mazer sword brooch and earrings set, gold wash with red, blue, and green rhinestones, accented with clear stones, brooch is 3¼" x 1½", earrings are 1⅛" x almost 1" long, only one earring is signed "Mazer." **$175.00 – 200.00.** Treasures-in-Time collection

Mazer Lucite fruit and clear rhinestones set in a gold-over-silver fur clip, 2" x 1⅝". **$300.00 – 350.00.** Treasures-in-Time collection

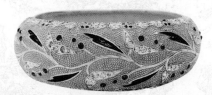

Joseph Mazer parure includes hinged bangle bracelet, earrings, and brooch, all gold plated, with enamel and hand-set rhinestones. **$750.00 – 800.00.** Treasures-in-Time collection

Regency pink rhinestone set of pin and earrings with large shaded pink drop, earrings are clip, signed "Regency" in capital letters on plaque on back of pin. **$200.00 – 240.00.** Treasures-in-Time collection

Austria japanned set of spray pin and earrings with clear rhinestones, all prong set. **$195.00 – 225.00.** Treasures-in-Time collection

Coppola e Toppo cuff bracelet with clear and pale green wired-on beads. **$550.00 – 600.00.** Treasures-in-Time collection

Pomé bracelet and earrings set in topaz. Design features three-quarter circle light topaz stones around round, darker topaz stones; 7" long. **$200.00 – 225.00.** Treasures-in-Time collection

Bellini speckled blue cabochon stones make up the design in this bracelet and earrings. Safety chain. **$100.00 – 125.00.** Treasures-in-Time collection

Eisenberg clip with clear emerald, marquise, and baguette rhinestones, accented with small clear stones. **$180.00 – 220.00.** Treasures-in-Time collection

Eisenberg crescent pin with large marquise and round rhinestones. **$140.00 – 160.00.** Treasures-in-Time collection

Florenza

Florenza jewelry has a style and design all its own, which makes it easily identifiable, even in a showcase filled with costume jewelry. The antique-looking settings and finishings give the jewelry a very Victorian look. The quality is apparent in the design and manufacture. Florenza used the highest-quality materials and rhinestones.

Beautiful large stones were often used as the centerpieces in the designs. Rhinestones of an inch or larger are common in Florenza designs, with colors reminiscent of the Victoria era.

Not all Florenza designs have a Victorian feel; they did stray from the concept infrequently. But one of the most amazing things about Florenza is the variety of items they designed and produced for ladies.

Picture frames and trinket boxes. Lipstick caddies (holders) and jeweled pillboxes. Ring holders and pincushions and jeweled ashtrays. Desk accessories and lighters and even saccharin holders, complete with tongs to lift out the tiny tablets.

Laurel Ladd Ciotti, owner of Eclecticla (www.eclecticala.com), adores Florenza and is a big collector. "I have little odds and ends of Florenza all over my house. My desk always has picture frames and trinket boxes by Florenza. I change them with the seasons. My dresser has Florenza lipstick holders and vanity items, and even my purse has a little jeweled Florenza pillbox filled with aspirin. I wouldn't want to go a day without looking at Florenza!" exclaims Ciotti. "I love the look," she continues, "It is elegant and charming and whether I am wearing Florenza or admiring the useful and unique household and vanity items in my collection, they always give me pleasure. I share what I can part with by putting items on my website under the heading "Fabulous Florenza" found at http://www.eclecticala.com/florenza/florenza.htm." Ciotti's pages devoted to Florenza showcase items for sale, and special items for viewing.

The Florenza name came from the owner's wife's name, Florence. Dan Kasoff started his costume jewelry company in the 1940s, but chose the name Florenza around 1950. Dan ran the company and was eventually joined by his son Larry. They ran the company together until 1981.

Florenza is currently a costume jewelry sleeper in the collecting field. Collectors who only want signed jewelry pay between $25.00 and $65.00 for the bolder larger designs. Other Florenza jewelry can be found for $5.00, $10.00, and $15.00.

Florenza desk accessories and vanity items seem to be priced according to how the dealer personally feels about the item. A trinket box with rhinestones decorating its removable lid may be priced as low as $20.00 by someone with an eye for fine china or porcelain. But a dealer in the costume jewelry may price the same box $75.00 or $85.00. I purchased my first Florenza trinket box for $25.00; it is a lovely piece with green cabochon rhinestones accented with sapphire blue rhinestones. The inside is lined with green felt. Another Florenza box was offered by the same dealer, but it only had a few pink rhinestones decorating it. When I asked the dealer why the other box was priced $80.00, she explained, "It's a much bigger box!"

Most of the collectors I have the opportunity to meet have a few pieces of Florenza jewelry in their collection. Florenza has some gorgeous cameo jewelry, which shows up in cameo collector's jewelry boxes. Florenza has portrait jewelry, such as a brooch that can be placed on the desk, it's folding stand attached to the back of the pin. So portrait jewelry collectors may own jewelry from the Florenza portrait jewelry line. And collectors of Victorian jewelry may be inclined to add a piece to their collections.

Laurel Ladd Ciotti has corresponded with Larry Kasoff in the past, as he visits her Florenza pages to view her current offerings. Ciotti says Mr. Kasoff is very pleased to see collectors seeking his family's jewelry and accessories.

More authors of costume jewelry books are covering Florenza, which means prices will inflate in the future. Now is the time to add some Florenza to your collection.

Topaz pin with black and amber cabochons, seed pearls and small topaz rhinestones. Large center stone is glass and open in the back. 2". I have also seen this exact pin with green stones and accented with chains and a tassel. **$45.00 – 50.00.** Author collection

Cameo bracelet, bangle with hand carved shell cameo. **$60.00 – 75.00.** Kim Paff collection

Courting couple brooch, cameo style, 2½" tall. **$45.00 – 50.00.** Author collection

Pocket watch vanity boxes, one pink, one blue, guilloche, they sit on three legs and have a Federal style eagle on the back, 2¼" long, very hard to find. **$75.00 – 90.00** each. Laurel Ladd Ciotti collection

Pair of pillboxes; round one has molded coral glass, tiny purse shaped box has faux turquoise and amethyst glass stones. Round pillbox, **$45.00 – 50.00**; tiny pocketbook, **$55.00 – 65.00.** Laurel Ladd Ciotti collection

Ring box with emerald green and rose rhinestones, faux pearls, and tiny glass pink beads. **$75.00 – 85.00.** Pink velvet pincushion with pink enameling and gold wash accents, **$85.00 – 95.00.** Laurel Ladd Ciotti collection

Pale blue velvet vanity accessories, all are marked "Florenza." Little pillbox has a poodle sitting on top, **$65.00 – 75.00.** Heart-shaped box, **$50.00 – 65.00.** Standing poodle pincushion has nodding head, **$65.00 – 75.00.** Laurel Ladd Ciotti collection

Lighter and frame. Lighter sits on four tiny legs and has a floral design all the way around, 2⅜" tall, also marked "Pereline" and "Japan," **$50.00 – 55.00.** Frame has pink and white mosaic tiles with a white gold wash, **$50.00 – 65.00.** Laurel Ladd Ciotti collection

This Federal-style brooch is also a stand-alone picture frame; photo shows one from the front and one from the back. The one on the left has the original Prince inset. **$125.00 – 145.00.** Laurel Ladd Ciotti collection

Fruits & Vegetables

Column #1:

One night as you surf the television channels you land on a collectibles show. An adorable little necklace of fruit shapes catches your eye. Or you page through a new jewelry book and see a parure of strawberry necklace, bracelet and earrings. It's love at first sight. Ah, a quest! We're off to find fruit jewelry!

It looks to be a cheap undertaking, doesn't it? How expensive can a necklace of plastic jewelry cost? Bring along your checkbook, with an unused line of credit, because you just might be in for a surprise. That fruit jewelry can set you back more than hundreds of dollars, some of it can set you back $1,000.00 or more.

Bakelite fruit salad jewelry appeals to both Bakelite collectors and fruit jewelry collectors. Prices climb quickly whenever quality pieces hit an auction block. A recent Dan Ripley Antiques auction featured a necklace and matching bracelet of Bakelite oranges, with green leaves, that brought a final price of $600.00. A red berry cluster pin with green leaves sold for $350.00, while a strawberries charm pin that had six carved berries with green painted crowns and leaves sold for $900.00.

Do these prices mean that the average collector cannot strive to add something fruity to their collection? Absolutely not. I recently found two fantastic necklaces at an auction to begin my personal collection of fruit jewelry. Both are extremely fun pieces. One features black glass beads along both sides with nearly life-size cherries, on stems, across the front. The other is a choker of strawberries with green leaves and large, gaudy, polka dot, brightly colored beads separating the strawberries. The price for the lot, which also included two necklaces I wouldn't be caught dead in, was $22.00.

My fellow collectors disagree vociferously about what fruit salad jewelry is, and what it isn't. Three of them came up with a "guide" for fruit salad jewelry that I would like to share with you. First, Elizabeth Nyland of Hudson, New York, describes what she thinks fruit salad IS: "1) A mix of the 'precious' gemstone colors — ruby red, emerald green, sapphire blue — leading to the look of a fruit salad made of a mix of fruit and their colors, shaped like fruit, grapes, strawberries, blueberries, etc. 2) With the stones 'carved' or molded — to depict leaves, flowers, and of course, fruit. 3) All set in 'platinum' colored settings — usually rhodium plated. 4) Surrounded by clear rhinestone pavé and sometimes baguettes too, but always totally jeweled with metal only being used to hold the stones, and not shown on its own. 5) Probably made in the 1930s and emulating the Cartier jewelry which was adapted from Indian jewelry. This is not to confuse it with the 'Jewels of India' by Trifari, which came later and was actually the name of specific collection(s)."

Pam Cobb in New Orleans, Louisiana describes what fruit salad is NOT: 1) set in gold tone, 2) non-carved stones in the "right" colors, 3) carved or molded stones in semi-precious stone colors, such as coral, turquoise and moonstones-type colors, 4) only ONE of the right colors. Deborah Parker in Virginia believes that "if you look closely at the individual molded glass stones, you can see that they resemble fruits. Sometimes they are shaped like flowers and leaves too, the important thing is that the piece contains 'fruits' and embodies a 'salad' that is a mix of colors." Thanks, ladies.

With these classifications, you can clearly see that there are differences between plain old fruit jewelry and fruit salad jewelry. But part of the fun of collecting is that it be just that, FUN. And what could be more fun than wearing one of the basic food groups around your neck or wrist?

Hollycraft lemon pin and earrings, both have enameled leaves with green and yellow rhinestones. **$150.00 – 165.00.**
Nancy Canās collection

Fruits & Vegetables

Column #2:

'Tis the season to be fruity, fa, la, la, la la ..... Happy Holidays! I bet you were expecting another Christmas tree jewelry column, but I have decided to try something different this holiday season. Fruit and vegetable jewelry. Yes, you read right!

Over the last decade of collecting, I have picked up a piece of fruit jewelry here and there. Until I started gathering it to prepare for this column, I didn't realize I was a fruit jewelry collector. I do remember all the searches online for cherries, pears, apples, strawberries, well, the list is nearly endless.

The Bakelite fruit jewelry is some of the most famous. Nearly every collector of vintage costume jewelry will know exactly what you are talking about when you mention the Bakelite cherries pins. There were a variety of designs, from carved logs with dangling cherries to a plain red bar pin with seven, nine or twelve cherries, and all included leaves.

A fun series came out of Austria in the 1950s called "Forbidden Fruit." It features Lucite fruit shapes encrusted with matching rhinestones. Apples, lemons, pears, limes, oranges, peaches and strawberries, along with watermelon, all types of berries and a nod to vegetables with tomatoes, carrots and eggplants.

Clusters of grapes came in a variety of colors; blue grapes with blue rhinestones, white grapes with green stones, black grapes with black stones, even pink grapes with white opaque rhinestones. Collectors are always discovering new color combinations. All the Forbidden Fruit have enameled green leaves. Search well before making a purchase, prices can be found for as little as ten dollars and as much as one hundred sixty five dollars. For the exact same pin.

Another line of fruit jewelry came from Austria around the same time period. It featured glass fruit, usually hanging from a branch with glass leaves and a rhinestone accent. Some stones were opaque, some transparent and others two-toned.

Molly Garza, owner of Le Bijouterie (www.rubylane.com/shops/lebijouterie) says the glass fruit signed "Made in Austria" or simply "Austria" is her favorite. "I recently sold a full parure, the twenty-two inch necklace, bracelet, brooch and tiny earrings, signed 'Made in Austria.' There were full of tiny citrus fruit with leaves, and very weighty for tiny fruit." Garza continues, "Fruit jewelry is beautiful. I have a Czechoslovakian pear fur clip on my website now that is full of the rich primary jewelry colored glass stones. The older pins are by far the most enticing to me. I also have a huge wood cherry brooch with the stems and leaves from the 1930s that garners a lot of attention because it is so enormous, and again, something that you rarely find."

Nearly every designer you can think of did something in fruit or vegetables. Chanel did grape clusters, resin cherries and enameled branches with glass fruit drops. Robert did a variety of enameled fruits and veggies like radishes, pears, strawberries, apples and tomatoes. Nettie Rosenstein must have liked apples, she added rhinestone drops to gold-tone apples with pavé rhinestones leaves.

BSK did a famous enameled watermelon with a pearl accent. Napier produced all types of charm bracelets with one, two or a basket full of fruits. The most desired Napier fruit bracelet is a very large, very heavy charm bracelet with a variety of glass bead fruits. Prices can reach two hundred dollars on this beauty, especially if you have the matching earrings. For fun fruit jewelry with a Spanish flair, seek out Isobel Canovas.

Of course Trifari, Weiss, Kramer, HAR, Boucher, Jomaz, Reja and Schiaparelli picked some fruit designs. Stanley Hagler and Christian Dior got into fruit jewelry designs in a BIG way. Do you remember Frank Hess, the famous Miriam Haskell designer? He did an extremely glamorous and colorful line of fruit and vegetable jewelry. His necklaces of silk, paté de verre and celluloid are highly coveted. One particular festoon necklace has a fabulous design in green and yellow. Upon closer inspection, you can see that the yellow and green "bead drops" are actually miniature corn on the cob beads!

Laurel Ladd Ciotti, owner of Eclecticala Vintage Jewelry (www.eclecticala.com) features her fruit jewelry under the heading "Sparkleberries." Not only apropos, but Ciotti informs me the sparkleberry is a real berry growing wild in Florida. Fruit and vegetable jewelry is so popular she can't keep it stocked. "As soon as I get it all stocked and looking nice again, inevitably, some collector comes along and buys most everything for their collection," states Ciotti. "The hottest item for me has always been cherries, then strawberries. Red fruits are king. I also have a lot of grape collectors. Grape pins appeal to not only the jewelry collector but also the wine collector. Western Germany fruit sets are very hot right now. Plastic is cool when it comes to fruit jewelry -- even regular old plastic, not just Bakelite.

"Collectors seem to look for colorful fruits rather than pastels or sterling type fruit pins so there are some good buys to be found in sterling fruit pins. Pineapples, pears and peaches are always in demand, as is anything unusual, like plums, blueberries and melons. Austrian fruit jewelry and the Lucite Forbidden fruits series are consistently in demand and bring the best prices lately. They are getting very hard to find!" she continues.

"Apples for teacher are a big seller in May and in December as parents buy them for gifts for their children's teachers. Pineapples are the symbol for hospitality and make a lovely hostess gift."

Ciotti concludes, "I like to wear several pieces of juicy fruit pins at once. People can't resist looking at them and I can actually see them start to salivate at the thought of tasty fruit. Aren't we lucky to be able to wear tasty fruit jewelry all year long?"

Many new items of fruit jewelry are being produced because of something called "Rockabilly." These . . . rockabillies . . . apparently love anything with cherries, as there is a profusion of new cherry jewelry available. Check around before buying a Bakelite cherry bracelet; the new designs are strikingly similar to the old designs.

Wear your fruit jewelry year round, but especially wear it at Christmas. 'Tis always the season to be fruity!

Unmarked grape brooch with large sapphire rhinestones; leaf and stem are decorated with clear rhinestones; from the 1940s. **$195.00 – 220.00.** Nancy Canãs collection

Stylized fruit with blue marquise stones, gold-tone leaves, 3¼" tall. **$75.00 – 95.00.** Laurel Ladd Ciotti collection

Kenneth Lane grape brooch, enameled green leaf with faux pearls. **$85.00 – 105.00.** Nancy Canãs collection

Coro melon stone brooch, with clusters of fruit or nuts, 3" long. **$75.00 – 95.00.** Laurel Ladd Ciotti collection

Green rhinestone pears pin, 2". **$40.00 – 50.00.** Laurel Ladd Ciotti collection

Warner strawberries, pin and earrings, deep red rhinestones. **$145.00 – 165.00.** Laurel Ladd Ciotti collection

Made in Austria white pears pin. **$55.00 – 65.00.** Laurel Ladd Ciotti collection

Coro white moonstone grapes fur clip. **$50.00 – 65.00.** Laurel Ladd Ciotti collection

Pastel moonstones grape cluster pin. **$45.00 – 55.00.** Laurel Ladd Ciotti collection

Coro blue ribbon and pastel moonstones pin. **$70.00 – 80.00.** Laurel Ladd Ciotti collection

Florida loquats enameled pin and earrings, 3" long. **$90.00 – 95.00.** Laurel Ladd Ciotti collection

Two-tone pineapple pin, 2½". **$35.00 – 40.00.** Laurel Ladd Ciotti collection

Pair of Coro blue moonstone pins. Smaller of the two, **$65.00 – 85.00**; blue ribbon one, **$45.00 – 55.00.** Laurel Ladd Ciotti collection

Watermelon rhinestone pin, nearly 2" long. **$50.00 – 75.00.** Laurel Ladd Ciotti collection

Made In Austria red rhinestone berry set of pin and earrings, both signed. **$125.00 – 145.00** set. Laurel Ladd Ciotti collection

Fruit salad pin, circa 1920, 2" x 1½".
$95.00 – 115.00. Laurel Ladd Ciotti collection

BSK corn in husk, pebble stones, nephrite chips, enamel and a pearl accent. **$65.00 – 75.00.**
Laurel Ladd Ciotti collection

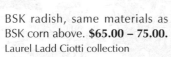

BSK radish, same materials as BSK corn above. **$65.00 – 75.00.**
Laurel Ladd Ciotti collection

ART walnut, enameled with a pearl accent. **$65.00 – 75.00.**
Laurel Ladd Ciotti collection

One smiling onion, one smiling red apple enameled pin. **$25.00 – 35.00** each.
Laurel Ladd Ciotti collection

Three different carrot pins, enameled, the single on the bottom right is signed "JJ." **$35.00 – 45.00** each. Laurel Ladd Ciotti collection

Googly-eyed yellow pear and green apple smiling pins. **$25.00 – 35.00** each. Laurel Ladd Ciotti collection

Red enameled JJ radish. **$40.00 – 45.00.**
Laurel Ladd Ciotti collection

Weiss enameled Indian corn, 3¼" long.
$85.00 – 105.00. Laurel Ladd Ciotti collection

Green rhinestone acorns, gilded
pot metal. **$65.00 – 75.00.**
Laurel Ladd Ciotti collection

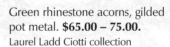

Made in Austria deep purple glass berries,
enameled leaves, C clasp, accented with
orange rhinestones **$65.00 – 75.00.**
Laurel Ladd Ciotti collection

HAR orange pin with opaque green rhinestone accent, part of a series. **$45.00 – 55.00.** Author collection

Flying Colors ceramic cherries necklace with ceramic beads, 16" long, barrel clasp, made by the Flying Colors Ceramic Jewelry Company in San Francisco, California. **$100.00 – 125.00.** Author collection

An amazing find, a carved Bakelite strawberry fur clip, over 2" long, no markings, metal is in excellent condition. **$400.00 – 450.00.** Author collection

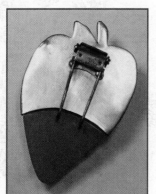

Reverse view of Bakelite strawberry fur clip.

Large pair of lemons enameled pin with rhinestone accents. **$55.00 – 65.00.** Author collection

Unusual set of matched pins from the Forbidden Fruit series, 1" round fruit with different colored rhinestones; the pins in this series usually have only one color of rhinestones. **$150.00 – 175.00** pair. Author collection

Pair of grapes earrings, white with blue rhinestones. **$85.00 – 95.00.** Author collection

White grapes pin with pale green rhinestones, one leaf is missing, still desirable. **$65.00 – 75.00.** If perfect, **$110.00 – 125.00.** Author collection

Photo showing pin and earrings together.

Very large strawberry rhinestone and enamel pin, over 2" long. **$55.00 – 65.00.** Author collection

Small enameled strawberry with stem attached, 1¼". **$10.00 – 12.00.** Author collection

Lisner bunch of grapes pin with large green rhinestones. **$40.00 – 45.00.** Author collection

This little crabapple pin has two ceramic apples on it, 1½" long. **$15.00 – 20.00.** Author collection

Beautifully enameled pear pin, 1¼". **$10.00 – 12.00.** Author collection

This enameled bunch of bananas pin is often mistaken for Bakelite, but the bananas are glass. 2" x 2". **$20.00 – 25.00.** Author collection

I'm still trying to figure out this mystery fruit, you be the judge. 2½" long, green glass fruit stone. **$15.00 – 20.00.** Author collection

Pair of pineapple earrings with sky blue stones, 1¼". **$20.00 – 25.00.** Author collection

Pair of pineapple pins, with sky blue stone. **$20.00 – 25.00.** Author collection

This fruit series is gaining popularity quickly, and prices have skyrocketed. The stones are all carved glass, except for the red rhinestone accent. Most are signed "Austria," and the stones are all prong set. **$30.00 – 50.00.** Author collection

Single apple pin with enameled leaf, less than 1" long, signed "Austria." **$25.00 – 40.00.** Author collection

The cherries on this pin are some type of molded plastic; with rhinestone accents, 2" long. **$20.00 – 30.00.** Author collection

Sarah Coventry apple pin slightly over 1", signed "Sarah-Cov" on stem. **$20.00 – 30.00.** Author collection

Pair of cherries pin with green and red rhinestones, cherries are very dimensional, rhinestones go all the way around, 1¾" long. Marked "MADE AUSTRIA." **$40.00 – 50.00.** Author collection

This bright red cherries or apples pin has a mark that is impossible to read, it could be "072" or "GTE" or "GTZ." 1½" long. **$35.00 – 40.00.** Author collection

De Nicola pearl fruit pin, enameled, almost 2" long. **$20.00 – 25.00.** Author collection

Back of De Nicola fruit pin.

Little enameled strawberry pin, 1½", with a big leaf. **$15.00 – 20.00.** Author collection

Hong Kong plastic pineapple necklace, extremely lightweight. Bunch of pineapples is almost 3" long, with large and small pineapples; pineapple chain is 26" long. **$10.00 – 20.00.** Author collection

This glass fruit pin is signed "Sarah Cov" with the copyright symbol, has a hook to add to a chain. Visible mark in stone is an air bubble. **$20.00 – 25.00.** Author collection

Weiss strawberry clip-on earrings, japanned, with red and green rhinestones, 1" long, one earrings is marked inside the back of the strawberry. **$75.00 – 100.00.** Author collection

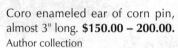

Coro enameled ear of corn pin, almost 3" long. **$150.00 – 200.00.** Author collection

Stanley rhinestone pear pin, almost 3" long. **$25.00 – 30.00.** Author collection

Bakelite, Lucite & Other Plastics

"In a recent online auction, an overpainted Bakelite figural ram with a moveable head sold for the remarkable price of $3,275.99. Bakelite collectors say there are several reasons the price of this piece skyrocketed. First, it was an unusual piece in that the head could be placed forward with the horns over the back of the ram's head, or facing downward giving the ram a butting appearance. The original brass pin holds the head on. Secondly, multi-color and laminated Bakelite items are not exactly rare, but they are not found as commonly as solid color items, so can have a higher value.

Thirdly, this piece was offered on an Internet auction. More collectors and sellers are discovering this to be a great place to buy and sell jewelry. Pieces that before would only be purchased by dealers and offered to a select few collectors are more readily available to the general public. Lastly, this was a piece that was driven up in price by the desire of several bidders to own it. It showed a trend in the recent past for very high prices of unusual Bakelite pieces."

When I first wrote those words in early 1997, online Internet auctions were still relatively new. Yet it is fascinating to see that all of the above information still holds true. A recent online auction offered a pair of cream and black Bakelite bangle bracelets, which I watched until the end. With fifteen minutes left, the pair was at $1,400.00; ten minutes left saw them at $1,500, a minute later they crept up to $1,700.00. When the dust settled, the bracelets had sold for over $6,000.00. It seems Bakelite is the one constant in the changing costume jewelry market.

Bakelite, the first modern plastic, was discovered by Leo Hendrik Baekeland in 1907, and patented in 1909. Scientists had been working with the phenol and formaldehyde combination that resulted in deposits of sticky mixture that refused to harden. Baekeland, bringing an entrepreneurial eye to the process, found a way to harden the product by "cooking" the substance in a chemical pressure cooker he called the "Bakelizer" which turned the gunk into a hard translucent moldable substance. He realized immediately that this new product might be good for everything from jewelry to billiard balls. And, jewelry collectors would say, "the rest is history."

If the current Bakelite market makes you want to plunge in and buy whatever you can find, take extreme caution. It takes skill and experience to recognize the difference between Bakelite, plastic, and Lucite. According to Karima Perry, owner of Plastic Fantastic (www.plasticfantastic.com), Bakelite can be brittle and fragile. Carefully inspect each piece before buying. Watch for cracks which will only worsen, scratches which permanently mar the finish, and loose, rusted or wobbly hinges or pin backs, which can cause major damage to a piece if they give way while you are wearing them.

Bakelite and Celluloid dangle necklace and matching pin, great condition, goes with any outfit. **$250.00 – 275.00.**
Kim Paff collection

Shultz bangle, white with red dots, pineapple cut, 2". **$450.00 – 475.00.**
Kim Paff collection

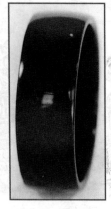

Shultz bangle, dark brown with paprika dots, 1". **$400.00 – 425.00.**
Kim Paff collection

Shultz bangle, confetti dot, 1½". **$800.00 – 850.00.**
Kim Paff collection

Shultz bangle, green checker-board, 1". **$800.00 – 850.00.**
Kim Paff collection

Shultz bangle, pistachio with rose dots, ⅝". **$275.00 – 295.00.** Kim Paff collection

Bakelite bangle, carved, overdyed, 1½". **$250.00 – 275.00.** Kim Paff collection

Bakelite bangle, butterscotch, sunflower carving, ⅞". **$400.00 – 425.00.** Kim Paff collection

Bakelite bangle, diamond cut, domed, 1¼". **$350.00 – 375.00.** Kim Paff collection

Bakelite 2" round, carved, and pierced floral pin. **$100.00 – 125.00.** Kim Paff collection

Bakelite five-piece set of dress clips, dark caramel, one large at 2⅝", four smaller at 2" each. **$120.00 – 175.00** set. Kim Paff collection

Bakelite carved African princess with rhinestones, overdyed black over butterscotch, 3¼". **$325.00 – 350.00.** Joan Redden collection

Bakelite carved cloak clasp, brown with gold filigree findings, 6". **$40.00 – 55.00.** Joan Redden collection

Trio of Bakelite crosses, 2¾", 3", and 3¼". **$100.00 – 125.00.** Kim Paff collection

Bakelite carved green dangle dress clip, wreath shape with dangle beads, 2½". **$110.00 – 120.00.** Kim Paff collection

Bakelite carved red anthurium dress clips, 2". **$75.00 – 85.00** pair. Kim Paff collection

Bakelite red confetti dot dress clip,
Moderne style, 2½". **$75.00 – 100.00.**
Kim Paff collection

Bakelite apple juice and black cameo on
tricolored Lucite chain. **$75.00 – 85.00.**
Kim Paff collection

Bakelite carved butter-
scotch dress clip, leaf pattern, 2½". **$60.00 – 70.00.**
Kim Paff collection

Bakelite carved orange leaf
dress clip, 1¾". **$25.00 – 30.00.**
Kim Paff collection

Bakelite carved root beer
dress clip, 1¾". **$45.00 –
50.00.** Kim Paff collection

Bakelite apple juice bead and dangle dress clip, 2¾". **$75.00 – 95.00.** Kim Paff collection

Bakelite fruit juice dangle bead necklace; apple juice, lime juice, and honey, on celluloid chain. **$140.00 – 160.00.** Kim Paff collection

Bakelite reverse carved beads with matching pendant, 17"; crystal hand-cut beads between carved beads. **$425.00 – 475.00.** Kim Paff collection

Bakelite Plus charm necklace with all vintage charms, newly created. **$400.00 – 425.00.** Kim Paff collection

Lucite cubes and spheres made of lime juice, cherry juice, and apple juice, 28". **$40.00 – 45.00.** Kim Paff collection

Bakelite, Lucite & Other Plastics

Newly created Bakelite Plus bracelets, with all vintage and color-matched Bakelite materials. **$90.00 – 150.00.**
VintageJewelryArtsAndAntiques.com

Newly created Bakelite Plus bracelets are individually themed. **$90.00 – 150.00.**
VintageJewelryArtsAndAntiques.com

Bakelite black Deco pin with rhinestones, C clasp. **$75.00 – 85.00.** Nancy Canãs collection

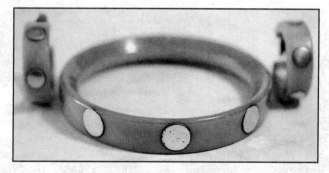

Bakelite bangle and clip earrings, pea soup with brass circular insets. **$125.00 – 150.00.** Nancy Canãs collection

Bakelite butterscotch faceted dress clips. **$75.00 – 85.00.**
Nancy Canãs collection

Lucite bracelet, a perfect match for jelly belly pins, unmarked. **$250.00 – 300.00.** Nancy Canás collection

KJL Lucite hinged bangle bracelet, clear with rhinestones. **$140.00 – 165.00.** Nancy Canás collection

KJL faux tortoise shell Lucite leaf with gold accent. **$75.00 – 95.00.** Nancy Canás collection

Kenneth Lane black Lucite dragonfly with clear and colored rhinestones. **$125.00 – 150.00.** Nancy Canás collection

KJL Lucite clamper bracelet with diagonal pattern clear rhinestones. **$140.00 – 165.00.** Nancy Canás collection

Kenneth Lane Lucite cuff bracelet in black, with clear rhinestones outlined in gold accents. **$125.00 – 140.00.** Nancy Canās collection

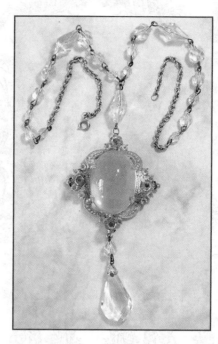

Schreiner Lucite pendant brooch, large Lucite cabochon centerpiece. **$250.00 – 275.00.** Nancy Canās collection

Close-up view of Schreiner pendant.

Bakelite reverse-carved apple juice bracelet and matching earrings. Nancy Canās collection

Bakelite reverse-carved brooch and pendant, same set. Parure with earrings and bracelet also, **$650.00 – 700.00.** Nancy Canās collection

Lucite orchid brooch in orange-yellow. **$75.00 – 95.00.**
Nancy Canās collection

Lucite orchid brooch in purple. **$110.00 – 125.00.** Nancy Canās collection

Lucite hand with dangling heart brooch, unmarked.
$100.00 – 125.00. Nancy Canās collection

Bakelite and celluloid necklace, red circles with Scottie dog heads.
$400.00 – 500.00. Nancy Canās collection

Close-up of Bakelite Scottie necklace.

Sculpted flower cuff bracelet, unmarked. Nancy Canãs collection

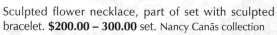

Side view of sculpted bracelet.

Sculpted flower necklace, part of set with sculpted bracelet. **$200.00 – 300.00** set. Nancy Canãs collection

Bakelite green dress clip with rhinestones, 2½". **$65.00 – 75.00.** Laurel Ladd Ciotti collection

Bakelite bangle, huge, 2¾", with large clear round rhinestones. **$325.00 – 500.00.**

Lucite green swirled pin with rhinestones, 3½". **$50.00 – 60.00.** Laurel Ladd Ciotti collection

Pink five-petal flower pin outlined with clear rhinestones. **$65.00 – 75.00.** Laurel Ladd Ciotti collection

Pink plastic turtle with blue shell and BIG eye. **$65.00 – 75.00.** Laurel Ladd Ciotti collection

Pink bouquet, with matching earrings and pink rhinestones, almost 4". **$65.00 – 75.00.** set. Laurel Ladd Ciotti collection

Lucite squared. Hinged bracelet in gold-tone. **$50.00 – 65.00.** Laurel Ladd Ciotti collection

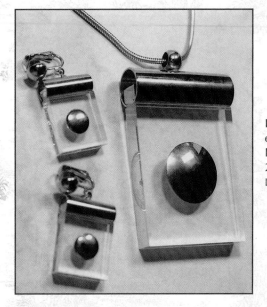

Lucite necklace and matching earrings in clear square Lucite, gold-tone. Necklace is 2½" x 2". **$75.00 – 85.00** set. Laurel Ladd Ciotti collection

Thermoplastic scallop shell in daffodil yellow with green rhinestones, almost 2½"; thermoplastic is opaque. **$75.00 – 85.00.** Laurel Ladd Ciotti collection

Pair of wooden horses, top one is hand carved and laminated, 2½", with glass eye; this was a piece of wooden tourist jewelry from Wyoming, circa 1965. The bottom one has a glass eye and red leather bridle leads and is 2½" x 2½". **$75.00 – 85.00** each. Laurel Ladd Ciotti collection

Bakelite red carved and pierced floral dress clip, transparent cherry juice, 2½". **$195.00 – 215.00.** Author collection

Wooden nodder pins, hand painted, on original cards, a pelican and a duck. **$15.00 – 20.00** each. Laurel Ladd Ciotti collection

Bakelite spring green Prystal carved dress clip, with a glass dome with reverse-carved and painted flowers in the center, 2½". **$195.00 – 215.00.** Author collection

Bakelite butterscotch criss-crossed dress clip, looks like a hedgehog, 2". **$75.00 – 85.00.** Author collection

Bakelite carved and resin washed creamed corn opaque clip, flower with pineapple carving, 1⅞". **$95.00 – 115.00.** Author collection

Bakelite transparent green with yellow swirls, 1⅝". **$50.00 – 60.00.** Author collection

Bakelite green clip, heavily and deeply carved, ⅜" x 1⅞". **$125.00 – 145.00.** Author collection

Bakelite deeply carved clips, matched pair of milk chocolate, lovely rib carving, 1¾" x ⅜". **$100.00 – 120.00.** Author collection

Bakelite clip, amazing; three-piece laminated black and apple juice; center is reverse carved and painted with flowers. 1¾". **$145.00 – 160.00.** Author collection

Bakelite clip, small oval cherry red with rhinestones, 1¼". **$45.00 – 55.00.** Author collection

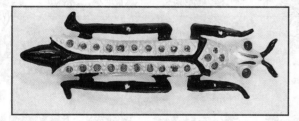

Celluloid cricket pin, 3", with red eyes and green rhinestones along his back, little dings on knees. **$200.00 – 225.00.** Author collection

Lucite transparent lavender fish pin, with rhinestones and gold-painted accents, over 2"; notice the big lips. **$40.00 – 45.00.** Author collection

Laminated bar pin with rhinestones, 3¼". **$45.00 – 50.00.** Author collection

Bakelite dress clips, matched pair with attached enameled rhinestone accents and a cat's eye, 2½". **$85.00 – 105.00** pair. Author collection

Spray of pink leaves accented with clear rhinestones, 4¾". **$65.00 – 75.00.** Author collection

Bakelite charm bracelet made of Bakelite balls in red and green and of disks in yellow, a fun and noisy piece, adjustable, 8½". **$195.00 – 215.00.** Author collection

Bakelite cherry red Prystal carved pin, 2½" x ½". **$140.00 – 160.00.** Author collection

Bakelite cherry red Prystal carved clip, 2" x ⅜". **$100.00 – 115.00.** Author collection

Bakelite lime Prystal clip, carved, 2½" x ¾" and up to ½". **$100.00 – 115.00.** Author collection

Large blue circle pin with blue rhinestones, nearly 3" diameter. **$10.00 – 15.00.** Author collection

Red circle pin with clear rhinestones, 2¼" diameter. **$10.00 – 15.00.** Author collection

White rickrack hollow bubble pin with colored rhinestones, dangling from small bar pin, quite colorful. **$35.00 – 45.00.** Author collection

Parures & Demi-Parures

Weiss necklace featuring added extension, matching earrings in clear rhinestones. **$125.00 – 140.00.** Kim Paff collection

Parklane red and white plastic necklace and dangle earrings on original card. **$35.00 – 40.00** set. Kim Paff collection

Parklane earrings on card.

BSK necklace, bracelet, and earrings, carved glass flower stones in shades of blue and green, with blue green rhinestones. Necklace, marked, 16"; bracelet, marked, 7"; earrings not marked. **$125.00 – 145.00.** Georgia Robinson collection

Hollycraft hinged cuff bracelet and earrings, emerald green stones and seed pearls, marked "Hollycraft" and "1954." **$150.00 – 165.00.** Georgia Robinson collection

Weiss looped ribbon pin and earrings, magenta and magenta aurora borealis stones. **$110.00 – 125.00.** Georgia Robinson collection

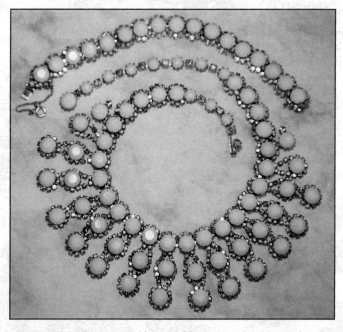

Kramer white festoon necklace and bracelet, white faceted stones with clear aurora borealis stones, necklace 15", bracelet 7½" x ½" wide. **$115.00 – 130.00.** Georgia Robinson collection

Coro Pegasus twisted rope medallion necklace and earrings, necklace is 17". **$200.00 – 250.00.** Georgia Robinson collection

Kramer floral medallion bracelet and earrings, accented with clear baguette stones. **$75.00 – 85.00.** Georgia Robinson collection

Hollycraft pin and earrings set, with pale blue aurora borealis stones and pearls, marked "COPR 1956." **$150.00 – 165.00.** Georgia Robinson collection

Judy Lee pink flower pin and earrings. **$55.00 – 75.00.** Georgia Robinson collection

Alice Caviness three strand beaded necklace and bracelet in lavender, amethyst, and pearl beads accented with rhinestones; necklace is 16½", bracelet is 7½" with a 1½" tasseled drop. **$300.00 – 350.00.** Georgia Robinson collection

Alice Caviness beaded necklace in red, blue, and green with a 2" pendant drop; necklace is 20", matching 3" earrings are not signed. **$150.00 – 195.00.** Georgia Robinson collection

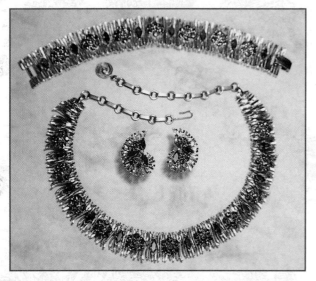

Lisner green parure of 17" necklace, 7" bracelet, and earrings.
$100.00 – 125.00. Georgia Robinson collection

Alice Caviness red glass tailored necklace and earrings; necklace is 22" long, signed on back of glass stone clasp; both earrings are signed. **$95.00 – 115.00.** Author collection

Alice Caviness red glass knotted bead necklace, 26", with matching earrings, same as preceding pair. Clasp is identical. **$75.00 – 95.00.** Author collection

Necklaces are perfect to wear together.

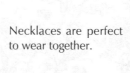

Alice Caviness opalescent bracelet and earrings, beautiful combination of beads, stones, and colors; notice pronged pearl clasp. Bracelet 7", earrings almost 2", all pieces marked. **$200.00 – 225.00.** Author collection

Alice Caviness hinged bangle bracelet with white and gold art glass beads. Beadwork reminiscent of Haskell. **$95.00 – 115.00.** Author collection

Reverse view of bracelet.

Close-up of earrings.

My favorite horse pin, he appears to be kicking his way to freedom. Looks like a heavy gold wash over sterling. The design is identical to the CoroCraft rearing horse, over 2". Unmarked, **$50.00 – 75.00**; if CoroCraft, **$200.00 – 225.00.** Author collection

You might be tempted to bypass these old plastic beaded sets from the 1950s, but this set proves that would be a mistake. The colors are bright and fresh, the wrap bracelet will fit almost any wrist, and the beaded earrings add a classic touch. You also might be surprised how good these sets look on. **$50.00 – 65.00.** Author collection

Close-up view of bracelet.

Not one piece in this amazing set is marked, but it is identical to an HAR set featured in another book. Bracelet is hinged on one side and has a safety chain. All stones are prong set; the workmanship and design is intricate and beautiful. **$300.00 – 325.00.** Author collection

Pin and earrings.

Adorable unmarked baby animal. Fawn? Calf? Pin and screw-on earrings, very well made, appears to be gold wash over sterling. I believe these are from the CoroCraft series of animal pins. Unmarked set, **$75.00 – 95.00**; if marked "CoroCraft," **$200.00 – 225.00** for the set. Author collection

Green carved and pierced faux jade pin and earrings marked "Newhouse," with floral motif. Pin is 1½"; earrings are 1", clip and screw on. All pieces are marked. **$25.00 – 35.00.** Author collection

Eisenberg Ice bracelet and earrings; bracelet 7" long, with a safety chain, all clear rhinestones. **$95.00 – 115.00.** Author collection

Tiny enameled pansy set, with pearl accents, screw-on earrings. **$20.00 – 35.00.** Author collection

Carved glass leaf pin and earrings; pin is 1¼" wide, earrings are clip on. **$25.00 – 35.00** set. Author collection

Vendôme multicolored necklace and earrings, a fun set; necklace is 24" long, with plastic beads. Square ones are painted pink, green spacer beads are crystal. Earrings are 1" clip on with a screw to tighten; only earrings are signed. **$150.00 – 165.00.** Author collection

Photo of pendant.

Photo of earrings.

Close-up of signature.

Jackie Collins pendant and earrings, original box for necklace, original card for earrings, 3¼" pendant drop with green and black cabochons and clear rhinestones, 32" chain; earrings are 2½" long, all pieces are marked. **$100.00 – 125.00.** Author collection

Napier seashell charm bracelet and earrings, bracelet 7". Very noisy set, but very fun, a great attention getter. Bracelet marked "Napier," earrings are marked "Napier Pat. Pend." **$100.00 – 125.00.** Author collection

Close-up of mark on necklace.

Barclay pastel set of necklace and pin, gold rope trimmed, snake chain. Necklace is 15" long, pin is 2", both marked. Shades of lavender, pale green, and pale blue. **$145.00 – 160.00.** Author collection

Close-up of pin.

Napier white plastic bead bracelet and earrings; bracelet is 7", earrings hang nearly 2½". All marked. **$75.00 – 90.00.** Author collection

Napier yellow glass and brass bracelet and earrings, 7" bracelet and 1½" earrings. Heavy and noisy. **$85.00 – 105.00.** Author collection

Norma sterling Dutch people, heads are a green stone, she is 2¼" high, he is 2⅓". Both are marked "Sterling" and "Pat. Pend," one is marked "Norma" in script, the other in block. **$175.00 – 225.00** pair. Laurel Ladd Ciotti collection

Sarah Coventry silver-tone crackle art glass in morning glory blue, includes bracelet, earrings, and ring. **$105.00 – 135.00.** Laurel Ladd Ciotti collection

Green and clear rhinestone set of bracelet, pin, and dangle earrings. Bracelet is 7". **$135.00 – 145.00.** Laurel Ladd Ciotti collection

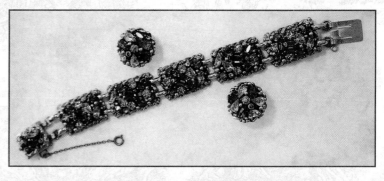

Barclay set of lavender and pale blue bracelet with safety chain and earrings. Bracelet is very heavy, 7½" long, earrings are 1" wide, and all pieces are marked. **$150.00 – 165.00.** Author collection

Close-up of bracelet.

Mark on back of earring.

142

Kramer of N.Y. blues and greens bracelet and earrings; bracelet is 7" long, earrings are 1½" and marked "Kramer." Silver-tone, all stones prong set. **$150.00 – 165.00.** Author collection

Jade set of necklace, bracelet, and earrings in original fabric box, all original tags. A beautifully crafted set from the Jade Dynasty Collection. **$100.00 – 135.00.** Author collection

Top of fabric box, coming slightly unglued.

Unsigned Sphinx set in the Mogul style, 1970s, jewel-tone bangle bracelet with matching earrings. **$285.00 – 305.00.** Laurel Ladd Ciotti collection

Unusual stretch bracelet in jonquil, ball cluster earrings. **$90.00 – 95.00.** Laurel Ladd Ciotti collection

Vendôme gold-tone leaf with clear stones, brooch and earrings, appears to be moving in the wind. **$130.00 – 180.00.** Laurel Ladd Ciotti collection

Red marquise spray set of pin and matching earrings, 2⅞" tall. **$85.00 – 95.00.** Laurel Ladd Ciotti collection

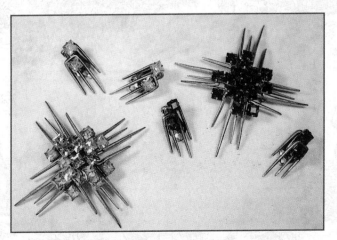

Atomic set on original card. Laurel Ladd Ciotti collection

Abstract atomic spray pins with matching earrings, reds and blues, pin is almost 3" long, funky set. **$60.00 – 65.00** set. Laurel Ladd Ciotti collection

Coro doorknocker with rose knocker and matching rose earrings, 2½". **$60.00 – 70.00.** Laurel Ladd Ciotti collection

Bow pin and earrings, pink flowers with green centers, pin is 2½" tall. **$90.00 – 95.00.** Laurel Ladd Ciotti collection

Coro Hibiscus pin and earrings in original box and card, with pink enameling. **$110.00 – 120.00** set. Laurel Ladd Ciotti collection

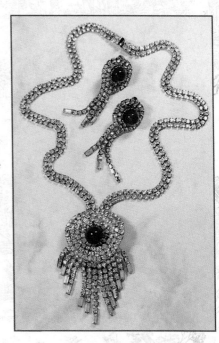

Green art glass pendant and earrings, 16" long, with 1½" drop; earrings are 2¼" long. **$145.00 – 155.00.** Laurel Ladd Ciotti collection

Unsigned set of gold-tone pear shapes necklace and earrings. **$125.00 – 130.00.** Laurel Ladd Ciotti collection

Nosegay of beaded flowers, 2" tall. **$75.00 – 80.00** pair. Laurel Ladd Ciotti collection

Lavender set of 16" necklace and matching earrings. **$125.00 – 140.00.** Laurel Ladd Ciotti collection

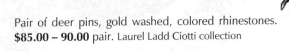

Pair of deer pins, gold washed, colored rhinestones. **$85.00 – 90.00** pair. Laurel Ladd Ciotti collection

Ledo seashells set with clear rhinestones, beautiful design. **$145.00 – 155.00.** Laurel Ladd Ciotti collection

Green glass dress clips on engraved back. **$85.00 – 90.00** pair. Laurel Ladd Ciotti collection

Gold-tone necklace and earrings, circa 1960s, with faux coral, ivory, and turquoise, on a snake chain, with rhinestone accents. Chain is 24" long. **$125.00 – 135.00.** Laurel Ladd Ciotti collection

Napier triple-chain necklace and bracelet with amethyst cushion stones, very heavy, signed "Napier" in block letters. **$125.00 – 135.00** set. Laurel Ladd Ciotti collection

Bib necklace with aqua rhinestones, circa 1930, wonderful patina, matching dangling earrings. **$195.00 – 225.00.** Laurel Ladd Ciotti collection

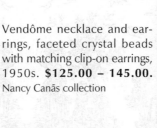

Vendôme necklace and earrings, faceted crystal beads with matching clip-on earrings, 1950s. **$125.00 – 145.00.** Nancy Canãs collection

Karu parure with prong-set stones in shades of purple, gold-tone. **$150.00 – 165.00.** Nancy Canãs collection

Trifari pin and earrings in matt silver with clear rhinestones. **$135.00 – 155.00.** Nancy Canãs collection

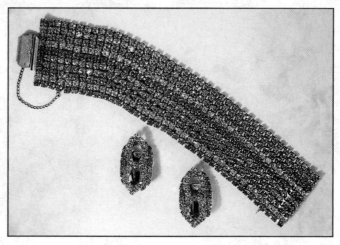

Unmarked set of pastel stones on gold-tone mesh, with clip earrings. **$150.00 – 170.00.** Nancy Canãs collection

Vendôme sculpted metal flower pin and earrings with gold plating, matching swinging ball earrings. **$145.00 – 165.00.** Nancy Canãs collection

Whiting & Davis faux turquoise parure, silver-tone mesh bracelet with fringe, adjustable ring, and matching earrings. **$140.00 – 170.00.** Nancy Canãs collection

Trifari pin and earrings, clear and sapphire rhinestones, rhodium plated. **$165.00 – 190.00.** Nancy Canãs collection

Coro star pin and earrings, rhodium plated, with blue rhinestones. **$75.00 – 85.00.** Nancy Canás collection

Unmarked emerald set from the 1940s, has clear stones and is rhodium plated. **$150.00 -175.00.** Nancy Canás collection

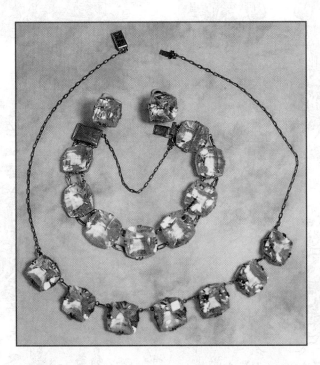

Sterling crystal parure in the Art Deco style, earrings are screw back. **$350.00 – 450.00.** Nancy Canás collection

Black faceted glass pin and earrings, pin has C clasp. **$55.00 – 70.00.** Nancy Canás collection

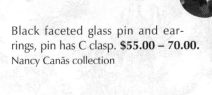

Back view of black glass pin, pin is signed "J.P."

Weiss set with large blue stones, silvertone, screw-on earrings. **$85.00 – 95.00.** Nancy Canās collection

Vendôme set of enameled holly leaves with red Lucite berries, accented with clear stones. **$125.00 – 165.00.** Nancy Canās collection

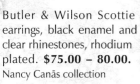

Butler & Wilson Scottie earrings, black enamel and clear rhinestones, rhodium plated. **$75.00 – 80.00.** Nancy Canās collection

Caterpillar scatter pins, illegible mark, could be Boucher and number, enameled with rhinestone eyes. **$50.00 – 65.00** each, **$175.00** set. Nancy Canās collection

Alice Caviness demi-parure, frosted petals rimmed in gold with clear stone accents. **$110.00 – 135.00.** Nancy Canās collection

Unmarked faceted black beads necklace, three strands. **$40.00 – 45.00.** Nancy Canās collection

Schreiner demi-parure, faux lapis stones, with magenta stones in a cross necklace with matching clip earrings. **$200.00 – 250.00.** Nancy Canās collection

Yves St. Laurent parure of necklace, bracelet, and ear clips; this set has gold-tone circular pebble discs. It is a limited edition, with the necklace and bracelet each being signed and numbered; earrings are not numbered. **$325.00 – 425.00.** Nancy Canās collection

Close-up of signature on bracelet.

Close-up of clasp on necklace.

Abalone shell necklace, bracelet, and earrings, souvenir jewelry from a trip to Mexico. **$150.00 – 200.00.** Minnie Lee Bounds collection

Necklaces

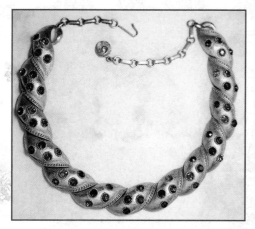

Lisner gold-tone link necklace with green, red, blue, and topaz stones, 1950s, links are 1" wide, necklace is 16" long. **$75.00 – 95.00.** Georgia Robinson collection

Coro necklace with aqua rhinestones and pearls, 16", even has aqua accents at the clasp. **$175.00 – 200.00.** Georgia Robinson collection

Miriam Haskell leaf necklace, with twisted gold chain and rhinestone chain, and rhinestone chain dangles, 14". **$375.00 – 450.00.** Georgia Robinson collection

Vendôme collar with large stones, silver-tone, reverse-faceted pear-cut stones, beautiful design. **$200.00 – 225.00.** Georgia Robinson collection

Alice Caviness two-strand beaded necklace, pale blue aurora borealis and pearl beads, two large center drops, beautifully designed to look like two necklaces. **$165.00 – 195.00.** Georgia Robinson collection

Bohemian-style citrine choker, enameled, unsigned. **$175.00 – 185.00.** Kim Paff collection

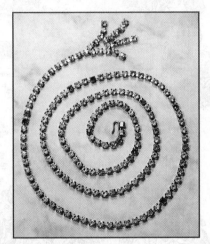

Unsigned lariat necklace, clear rhinestones, 36". **$75.00 – 85.00.** Kim Paff collection

Monet gold-tone chunky necklace with original box, articulated 3" medallion. **$120.00 – 130.00.** Kim Paff collection

Alice Caviness three-dimensional choker, rhinestones and white and black pearls. **$245.00 – 265.00.** Kim Paff collection

Unsigned black art glass bead and chain necklace with a gold flower medallion that has a black glass center, 20" long. **$40.00 – 45.00.** Kim Paff collection

Miriam Haskell pearl choker, long fluted pearl beads with rondelles, Miriam Haskell hang tag. **$175.00 – 195.00.** Kim Paff collection

Unsigned black glass faceted two-strand choker with gold and black faceted beads. **$45.00 – 50.00.** Kim Paff collection

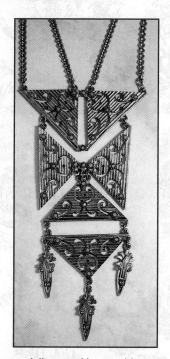

Medallion necklace, gold-tone, double chain, segmented scroll cut design with faux turquoise stones. **$75.00 – 85.00.** Nancy Canās collection

Unsigned red faceted glass bead necklace, 1930s, graduated beads. **$85.00 – 105.00.** Nancy Canās collection

Trifari dangle necklace, silver-tone with moonstone clusters, 15". **$160.00 – 175.00.** Patti Collins Bultman collection

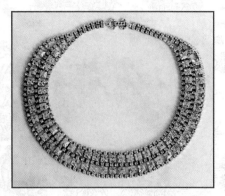

Clear rhinestone collar, in square and round stones, 15". **$175.00 – 185.00.** Patti Collins Bultman collection

Kenneth Lane hand necklace, gold-tone, two chains, two birds and flowers in center, 30". **$140.00 – 175.00.** Patti Collins Bultman collection

Close-up of hand detail.

Monet gold-tone square and rectangle necklace, marked on necklace and has attached hang tag. **$150.00 – 175.00.** Patti Collins Bultman collection

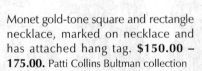

Napier stylized sea serpent necklace, chain is 15", sea serpent is 5" x 3". **$175.00 – 250.00.** Patti Collins Bultman collection

Miriam Haskell glass bead necklace in black, silver, and pewter, 70" long, Miriam Haskell hang tag. **$140.00 – 160.00.** Patti Collins Bultman collection

Miriam Haskell necklace, from the Sticks and Stones series, wood square beads, simulated sea glass, shells and coral, 30". **$100.00 – 140.00.** Patti Collins Bultman collection

Miriam Haskell Bakelite Asian pendant, gold-tone, with hangtag, 30" long. **$150.00 – 200.00.** Patti Collins Bultman collection

Portrait necklace, 27" chain, three dangles on pendant, probably Florenza but not marked. **$95.00 – 105.00.** Laurel Ladd Ciotti collection

Flapper necklace, pearls with rhinestone beads, very heavy, 60" long. **$125.00 – 135.00.** Patti Collins Bultman collection

Bohemian glass necklace in fire engine red, no clasp, made to slip over wearer's head, circa 1925, brass, 23½" long. **$90.00 – 105.00.** Laurel Ladd Ciotti collection

Large blue glass stone pendant, circa 1925 – 1935, probably European. **$85.00 – 125.00.** Laurel Ladd Ciotti collection

Miriam Haskell butterfly necklace, 16" long, turquoise-colored beads, beautiful detailing on butterflies. **$295.00 – 495.00.** Laurel Ladd Ciotti collection

Coro necklace with slide on snake chain, circa 1947.
$60.00 – 75.00. Laurel Ladd Ciotti collection

Brass filigree necklace with French jet; notice the lovely chain. **$60.00 – 75.00.** Laurel Ladd Ciotti collection

Miriam Haskell necklace from Sticks and Stones series, made up of plastic faux coral and glass faux turquoise sticks and stones, 27" long, signed on clasp and hang tag. **$100.00 – 145.00.** Laurel Ladd Ciotti collection

Unmarked blue rhinestone necklace with blue art glass bead accents, 16" long. **$55.00 – 75.00.** Author collection

Brania eight-strand plastic bead necklace; decorative clasp has all glass stones and rhinestones, push-in clasp is worn hanging to the side, not in the back. Mimi di N, designed for Brania. Rare. **$250.00 – 275.00.** Author collection

Reinad rhinestone pendant on 14½" chain, multiple colors and shapes of stones, all stones except for the small round ones are foiled, prong set, and open in the back. **$160.00 – 170.00.** Author collection

The bird on this necklace has a bit of attitude, so he is hereby called "Mr. Jaybird." He probably was born in the 1940s, has cloisonné enameling on his mesh body, and his slide is adjustable, with tiny cork inserts. His chain is 24" long, and the slide has tiny bead accents. My husband sneaked back into the antique store to buy him for me. Romance after twenty-five years of marriage. **$125.00 – 150.00.** Author collection

Pendant of tiny blue seashells, white beaded flowers, and clear rhinestone accents are reminiscent of Haskell and Robert work. **$50.00 – 65.00.** Author collection

Bracelets

All bracelets in this section are 7", unless stated otherwise.

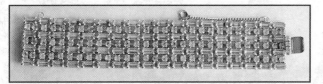

Weiss bracelet in clear stones, 1¼", slide in clasp. **$135.00 – 145.00.** Patti Collins Bultman collection

Christian Dior for Kramer red art glass bracelet with clear stone accents and a safety chain. **$85.00 – 125.00.** Laurel Ladd Ciotti collection

Erwin Pearl silver-tone link bracelet, very comfortable design, 7¼". **$45.00 – 55.00.** Laurel Ladd Ciotti collection

Big gold link bracelet, five segments, prong-set colored stones with atomic prongs, clear stones in leaves, floral design, 1¼" x ½". **$160.00 – 175.00.** Laurel Ladd Ciotti collection

Victorian Revival cuff bracelet with amethyst stones and pearls, safety chain. **$325.00 – 400.00.** Laurel Ladd Ciotti collection

Side view of Victorian Revival bracelet.

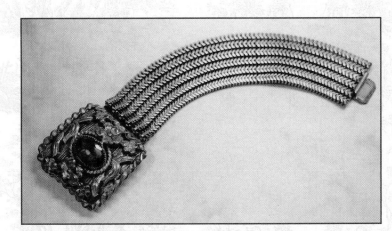

Victorian Revival flexible link bracelet, circa 1940, blue cabochon in link clasp. **$65.00 – 75.00.** Laurel Ladd Ciotti collection

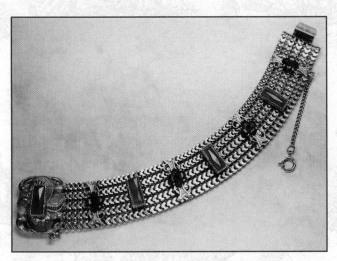

Victorian Revival bracelet with green and red molded stones, gold-tone. **$185.00 – 195.00.** Laurel Ladd Ciotti collection

Blue beaded bracelet with a rhinestone ball drop, very feminine design. **$55.00 – 65.00.** Laurel Ladd Ciotti collection

Bracelets

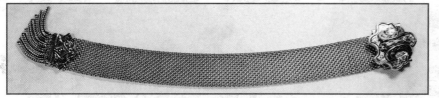

Marino Victorian Revival bracelet with chain dangles on the end. **$65.00 – 80.00.** Laurel Ladd Ciotti collection

Victorian Revival link bracelet with green and yellow rhinestones. **$50.00 – 65.00.** Laurel Ladd Ciotti collection

Rebajes sterling bracelet, articulated cuff style, heart design, 2". **$150.00 – 170.00.** Kim Paff collection

Miriam Haskell pearl bracelet with pastel rhinestones and silver filigree, signed. **$150.00 – 200.00.** Kim Paff collection

Sherman bracelet, gray, champagne and topaz stones, each link is comprised of two marquise and one round stone making this bracelet extremely fluid. **$180.00 – 220.00.** Georgia Robinson collection

Whiting & Davis cuff bracelet, chrome with black inserts. **$95.00 – 105.00.** Nancy Canãs collection

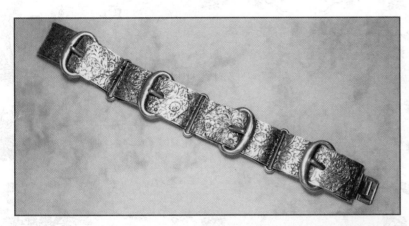

Napier Art Deco silver buckle bracelet with a floral design and four buckles; the design continues on the back of the bracelet. **$165.00 – 195.00.** Nancy Canãs collection

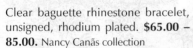

Clear baguette rhinestone bracelet, unsigned, rhodium plated. **$65.00 – 85.00.** Nancy Canãs collection

Kenneth Jay Lane zebra clamper, enameled with clear rhinestones. **$125.00 – 165.00.** Nancy Canãs collection

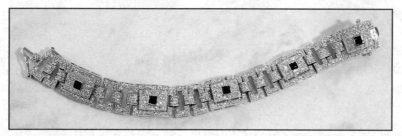

Art Deco silver-tone bracelet with clear and sapphire rhinestones, mimics the real thing. **$225.00 – 250.00.** Nancy Canãs collection

Kenneth Lane hinged bangle, enameled with red stones. **$130.00 – 160.00.** Nancy Canãs collection

KJL hinged bangle, large square stones in the front, not for the meek. **$135.00 – 165.00.** Nancy Canãs collection

McClelland Barclay sterling bracelet with a grape motif. **$300.00 – 350.00.** Nancy Canãs collection

Close-up of McClelland Barclay mark.

Bracelet in silver-tone, very large blue cabochons with clear and pale blue stones. Riveted in back of each link. Some collectors think this is a Juliana bracelet because of the five-link construction, but Frank DeLizza states it is not one of his designs. **$55.00 – 70.00.** Author collection

Elise '88 impressive multi colored rhinestone cuff bracelet, each stone is prong set and attached to the cuff base. Elise was a designer in the 1980s for a company called Pididdly Links, Ltd. who is still in business, but with a completely different line of jewelry. Pididdly Links, Ltd. started in business in 1969 in Lake Katrine, New York. These bracelets sold for more than $200.00 when new. Rare. **$250.00 – 325.00.** Author collection

KJL enameled seahorse hinged bangle, a truly beautiful design, accented all over with clear rhinestones, from his line for QVC in the early 1990s. This jewelry was packaged in a little red cloth pouch that says "K· J· L by Kenneth Jay Lane." **$200.00 – 225.00.** Author collection

Napier faux jade elephants, from its Oriental line of jewels that included bracelets with Oriental symbols and figures. These bracelets are difficult to find without the elephants' tusks being broken off, as the elephants are made of glass. Rare. **$165.00 – 185.00.** Author collection

Heavy gold-tone hinged bangle with two rows of invisibly set clear stones. **$20.00 – 30.00.** Author collection

Gold-tone hinged bangle with green marquise stones and clear round stones.
$20.00 – 30.00. Author collection

ART pearl hinged bangle with a safety chain.
$45.00 – 55.00. Author collection

Pearl and rhinestone bracelet with push-in clasp, silver-tone. **$40.00 – 55.00.** Author collection

Weiss green square rhinestone bracelet in gold-tone, with push-in clasp. **$40.00 –
45.00.** Author collection

Pale blue rhinestone bracelet with baguette center stones, offset by round paler blue
stones, push-in clasp with one stone on top. **$55.00 – 65.00.** Author collection

Bumblebee link bracelet in gold-tone, with large topaz stones, top of each bee has a little halo. Large fold-over clasp. **$95.00 – 125.00.** Author collection

Karu Arke Inc. pinks bracelet, some stones aurora borealis finish, fold-over clasp, bracelet is signed on back of second stone from the fold-over. **$75.00 – 85.00.** Author collection

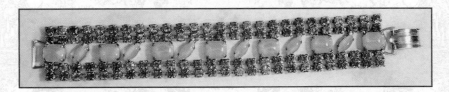

Shades of green rhinestone bracelet, large fold-over clasp. **$45.00 – 65.00.** Author collection

Rhinestones link bracelet in primary colors with white enameling accents; large center stones are open in the back. Fancy push-in clasp, gold-tone. **$80.00 – 90.00.** Author collection

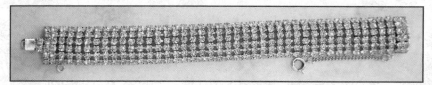

Alice Caviness clear rhinestone bracelet, 7¼" x ¾", silver-tone, safety chain, push-in clasp with two rhinestones on top. **$110.00 – 125.00.**
Author collection

Large green glass stones in gold wash over sterling bracelet, marked "Sterling" on back of first round stone, fold-over clasp has been poorly replaced, so signature (if signed) was lost forever. Beautiful bracelet is ½". **$95.00 – 115.00.** Author collection

Pink and purple rhinestones with art glass cabochons, square watermelon stones mounted upside down, all other stones are prong set, silver-tone with a safety chain and push-in rhinestone clasp, could be an unmarked Schreiner. **$110.00 – 135.00.** Author collection

Eisenberg clear rhinestone bracelet, crescent rhinestone accents, safety chain, push-in clasp that disappears. **$75.00 – 95.00.** Author collection

Well-made blue square rhinestone bracelet in gold-tone, stones are foiled and open in the back, fold-over clasp. **$30.00 – 40.00.** Author collection

Large round clear rhinestone bracelet in silver-tone, stones are foiled and open in back, push-in clasp goes into the end rhinestone and disappears. **$55.00 – 75.00.** Author collection

Wrapped link bracelet with a variety of green rhinestone colors and shapes, large fold-over clasp with scroll. **$80.00 – 95.00.** Author collection

Reinad gold-tone mesh bracelet with pearls, pink stones and faux blue cabochons, glass beads along sides, fold-over clasp. Rare. **$110.00 – 125.00.** Author collection

Pink disk bracelet in gold-tone, each disk is individually framed; bracelet adjusts to up to an 8" wrist. It is not marked but was purchased in a little box marked "Castlecraft." Castlecraft jewelry is rare. **$45.00 – 65.00.** Author collection

Photo of Castlecraft box.

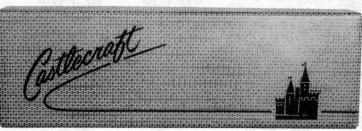

Weiss bracelet with blue rhinestones and gray pearls dangling, safety chain. **$75.00 – 95.00.** Author collection

Purple bracelet, five links, large cabochon center stones, some flecked with gold, pink rhinestones, fold-over clasp. **$125.00 – 165.00.** Author collection

Back view ofbracelet.

Crystal bead bracelet with rhinestone clasp. **$40.00 – 50.00.** Author collection

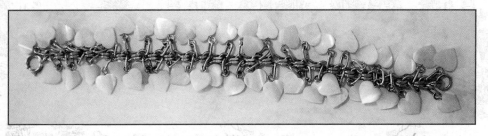

Mother-of-pearl heart charm bracelet, gold-tone, two hearts in each link. **$40.00 – 45.00.** Author collection

Coro Tree of Life charm bracelet with blue and pearl beads. **$40.00 – 45.00.** Author collection

Kramer hinged bangle with black rhinestones and a safety chain, very heavy. **$90.00 – 105.00.** Author collection

Lucite barrel beads bracelet with white glass beads, fold-over clasp. **$25.00 – 35.00.** Author collection

Pop beads bracelet. Pop beads from the 1950s still have a following today. Pop beads came in every color of the rainbow, even gold and silver, in glossy and matte finish. They came with findings to allow you to make multiple strand necklaces and bracelets. They are addictive. **$5.00 – 10.00** per strand; more for unusual colors such as vivid orange. Author collection

Unpopped pop bead, showing popped-off finish, and the "clasp" that makes them pop. Once you pop . . .

Vendôme three-strand gold-tone bracelet with green glass beads and blue rhinestone rondelles, pine cone gold beads, separated by gold links, marked on fold-over clasp. **$65.00 – 70.00.** Author collection

Napier jelly bean bracelet, plastic moonglow beads, medium fold-over clasp, signed in block letters. **$100.00 – 125.00.** Author collection

Pastel rhinestone bracelet, has a fold-over clasp marked "Coro" that does not appear to be original to the bracelet; priced as unsigned. **$40.00 – 45.00.** Author collection

Blues bracelet with large centerpiece design, silver-tone with safety chain. **$75.00 – 85.00.** Author collection

Judy Lee large pearl bracelet in silver-tone, with a safety chain, hang tag with signature, fold-over clasp. **$65.00 – 85.00.** Author collection

Close-up view of signature tag.

Miriam Haskell glass pearl bracelet in champagne colors, with signature rhinestone clasp. **$175.00 – 250.00.** Author collection

View of back of Haskell bracelet.

Miriam Haskell milk glass bead bracelet with elaborate beaded clasp. **$100.00 – 120.00.** Author collection

Brooches & Pins

Trifari Sterling coronation piece, crown on top, large blue center stone, 2½". **$295.00 – 325.00.** Laurel Ladd Ciotti collection

Large gray pearl flower spray brooch, gold-tone, 4½" x 3". **$135.00 – 145.00.** Laurel Ladd Ciotti collection

Kramer sterling key pin, 2½". **$75.00 – 85.00.** Laurel Ladd Ciotti collection

Weissco NY brooch with pendant bale; aqua, teal, and clear rhinestones; 3¼" x 3". **$155.00 – 175.00.** Laurel Ladd Ciotti collection

ART purple, pink, and clear stylized star pin, 2½" x 2½". **$65.00 – 80.00.** Laurel Ladd Ciotti collection

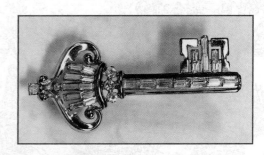

Trifari gold-tone key with clear round and baguette rhinestones, marked "Pat. Pend." and "Trifari." **$125.00 – 135.00.** Laurel Ladd Ciotti collection

Kramer round pin with clear rhinestones, 2⅓", variety of stone shapes. **$85.00 – 95.00.** Laurel Ladd Ciotti collection

Coro sterling mask fur clips, 1½" x 1¾". **$125.00 – 140.00** each. Laurel Ladd Ciotti collection

Coro doorknocker pin with gemstone. **$60.00 – 75.00.** Laurel Ladd Ciotti collection

Dress clip with clear rhinestones in different shapes, 2¾". **$80.00 – 90.00.** Laurel Ladd Ciotti collection

Unmarked, attributed-to-Schreiner brooch with pink, green, and blue cabochons, pearls, and colored stones, 3¼". **$140.00 – 160.00.** Laurel Ladd Ciotti collection

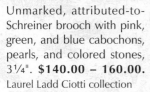

This brooch with tiny gray pearls and clear and black rhinestones is almost 2", with a highly domed back that is as pretty as the front. **$60.00 – 70.00.** Laurel Ladd Ciotti collection

Trifari enameled red flowers in a basket. **$55.00 – 75.00.** Laurel Ladd Ciotti collection

Sterling crown with red, blue and green stones, 1½", part of a set in which pieces could be attached to one another; set had a scepter and a saber. **$75.00 – 85.00.** Laurel Ladd Ciotti collection

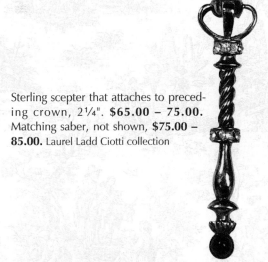

Sterling scepter that attaches to preceding crown, 2¼". **$65.00 – 75.00.** Matching saber, not shown, **$75.00 – 85.00.** Laurel Ladd Ciotti collection

Clock dangle pin with red stones and pearls, 2". **$40.00 – 45.00.** Laurel Ladd Ciotti collection

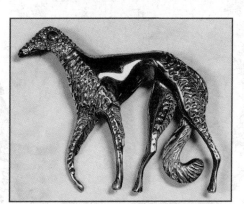

Sterling Art Deco Borzoi dog pin, almost 3". **$125.00 – 175.00.** Laurel Ladd Ciotti collection

NE in wine glass–marked dress clip with pastel fluted stones, 2". **$55.00 – 65.00.** Laurel Ladd Ciotti collection

Blue stone brooch in silver-tone with unfoiled stones, 1½". **$45.00 – 55.00.** Laurel Ladd Ciotti collection

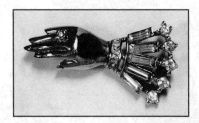

Trifari hand clip with clear rhinestones, marked "COPR" and "Sterling," hand is wearing a rhinestone ring, 1⅓". **$60.00 – 70.00.** Laurel Ladd Ciotti collection

Boucher Siamese fighting fish pin, enameled in white and blackish blue, also signed with "4811." **$65.00 – 80.00.** Laurel Ladd Ciotti collection

Coral shrimp with green eyes and clear rhinestones; piece has been copied recently. Vintage, **$75.00 – 85.00.** Laurel Ladd Ciotti collection

Stag brooch, enameled and japanned, with a green eye, rhinestones covering back. **$45.00 – 55.00.** Laurel Ladd Ciotti collection

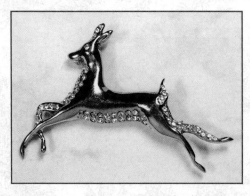

Deer pin in sterling vermeil with clear rhinestones. **$85.00 – 95.00.** Laurel Ladd Ciotti collection

Deer pin with large blue stone ears, almost 3½". **$125.00 – 135.00.** Laurel Ladd Ciotti collection

Green-eyed fox with red mouth is wearing a black collar. Silver-tone. **$45.00 – 50.00.** Laurel Ladd Ciotti collection

Little red-headed fox with gray body, red eyes, and black nose. **$45.00 – 50.00.** Laurel Ladd Ciotti collection

Mask pin wearing green dangle earrings, has a large jonquil stone. **$75.00 – 85.00.** Laurel Ladd Ciotti collection

Mask pin in silver-tone, blue stone in turban. **$50.00 – 60.00.** Laurel Ladd Ciotti collection

Mask pin with clear pavéd rhinestones, expressive mouth; she's got something to tell you. **$125.00 – 135.00.** Laurel Ladd Ciotti collection

Mask with blue stones, red lips. She wants you to tell her something. **$135.00 – $145.00.** Laurel Ladd Ciotti collection

Set of blackamoor pins. Nubian with gold-tone turban, **$40.00 – 50.00.** Earrings in silver-tone, **$30.00 – 40.00.** Pin with large red mouth, **$40.00 – 45.00.** Laurel Ladd Ciotti collection

Scarecrow and squirrel pins; scarecrow has a pearl head, and chain dangles for movement; marked "Em.J," for Emmons Jewelry. **$55.00 – 65.00.** Enameled squirrel in pewter with a green eye is marked "Gerry's," **$25.00 – 35.00.** Squirrel with rhinestone jacket and red eyes, **$45.00 – 50.00.** Laurel Ladd Ciotti collection

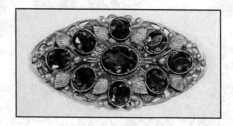

Brass pin circa 1930, with blue glass stones, gilded brass, 3¾". **$100.00 – 115.00.** Laurel Ladd Ciotti collection

Grape leaf sash pin with faux buckle, gently whitewashed on brass for summer wear, C clasp. Sash pins have a wider, sturdier clasp and often have the fake buckle motif. **$85.00 – $95.00.** Laurel Ladd Ciotti collection

Latticework brooch, stamped, with blue stones, circa 1930. **$65.00 – 75.00.** Laurel Ladd Ciotti collection

Sterling tiger lily brooch, trombone clasp, clear and black rhinestones. **$65.00 – 85.00.** Laurel Ladd Ciotti collection

Quiver pin, en tremblant strawflowers, enameled and gilded with purple stones, 1930s, pictured in the Sears Roebuck catalog. **$85.00 – 95.00.** Laurel Ladd Ciotti collection

Victorian Revival chatelaine, hollow gold-washed brass fur clips, circa 1930s – 1940s. **$115.00 – 125.00.** Laurel Ladd Ciotti collection

Chatelaine circa 1940, lock and key, even keyhole; alas, key doesn't work. Locket is hollow, prong-set red stones. Marked "LINC 12 kt. gf," (for 12 kt. gold filled.) **$85.00 – 95.00.** Laurel Ladd Ciotti collection

José Rodriguez set of three parrots. All are marked with the letter S within a star, and "Made in the USA." Patent information shows that Rodriguez (who was a Cuban immigrant) received this patent in 1940. All of his designs are related to the tropics. Each enameled and gold-washed pot metal bird is slightly different. **$95.00 – 135.00** each. Laurel Ladd Ciotti collection

"Made in USA" and S in a star marks hummingbird with a yellow throat, beautiful enameling. **$75.00 – 85.00.** Laurel Ladd Ciotti collection

Pink bird of paradise, has the Boucher enameling but not the Boucher mark, 5⅜". **$300.00+.** If signed Boucher, then **$1,200.00.** Laurel Ladd Ciotti collection

Unmarked pink birdies, same as Boucher, with moonstone eggs, 3½". **$500.00 – 525.00.** Laurel Ladd Ciotti collection

Trifari blue bird in nest with pearl eggs. **$45.00 – 50.00.** Laurel Ladd Ciotti collection

Bird of paradise pins, glass stones, pot metal, from the 1930s, unsigned. **$85.00 – 95.00** each. Laurel Ladd Ciotti collection

Unmarked enameled owl in flight pin; Coro has the exact same owl, designed in 1938 by Robert Geissmann. Blue rhinestone head. **$350.00 – 375.00.** Laurel Ladd Ciotti collection

Prototype for Boucher, pot metal, unsigned, green and blue enameling on body, yellow and black enameling on head. **$400.00+.** Laurel Ladd Ciotti collection

Rooster pin in gold-tone, hand-stamped design; very three dimensional, with his tail feathers cocked up and over. 3½". **$60.00 – 65.00.** Laurel Ladd Ciotti collection

Unsigned yellow peacock with flowers pin, circa 1960s. **$65.00 – 75.00.** Laurel Ladd Ciotti collection

Peacock with blue moonstones on his feathers, enameled body and feet; an unmarked Coro design. **$55.00 – 65.00.** Laurel Ladd Ciotti collection

Sterling peacock with pale amethyst stones, teal blue enameling on tail feathers. **$75.00 – 85.00.** Laurel Ladd Ciotti collection

Coro birds in flight, one pink, one brown, pot metal, rhinestones and enameling, also marked "Pat. Pend.," very three dimensional. **$175.00 – 200.00** each. Laurel Ladd Ciotti collection

Coro cockatiel in pink, standing on a pail of rhinestone flowers, hand-painted topknot, 2¾". **$125.00 – 150.00.** Laurel Ladd Ciotti collection

Réja Mr. Gander pin, sterling with vermeil, blue belly, dressed to go out on the town. There was also a Mrs. Goose to accompany him. He's off to town; she's at the feed and seed. Circa 1945. **$245.00 – 265.00.** Laurel Ladd Ciotti collection

Unmarked angry parrot, orange and green; could be a José Rodriguez design, due to vibrant colors and tropical subject. **$85.00 – 95.00.** Laurel Ladd Ciotti collection

Big-eyed chick with big mouth, too, possibly sterling with gold vermeil; maybe a duck, I'll have to ask him. **$150.00 – 165.00.** Laurel Ladd Ciotti collection

Pelican pin with enameling and rhinestones, circa 1940, beak and feet are yellow with black accents, pot metal. **$150.00 – 175.00.** Laurel Ladd Ciotti collection

This pair of pelican pins with a chain came in a box with the original owner's note saying, "Christmas Gift, December 22, 1947, Liberal, Kansas." Red and black enameling with clear rhinestones. **$60.00 – 70.00.** Laurel Ladd Ciotti collection

Pelican marked with an *S* in a star and "Made in USA," red and black enameling, 3", pot metal. **$90.00 – 105.00.** Laurel Ladd Ciotti collection

Flamingo in flight pin, pink enameling, marked "CARVEN" and "#1244." **$95.00 – 105.00.**
Laurel Ladd Ciotti collection

Flamingo with pink moonstone cabochons and clear rhinestones, has pretty little feet, pink and black enameling. **$125.00 – 140.00.**
Laurel Ladd Ciotti collection

Flamingo with marcasites, gilded pot metal, pink, white, and black enameling. **$85.00 – 95.00.** Laurel Ladd Ciotti collection

Unsigned pink flamingo, large pink stones, pink and white enameling, pot metal. **$85.00 – 95.00.**
Laurel Ladd Ciotti collection

Flamingo with a pink eye, pot metal, pink, black, and white enameling, circa 1940. **$95.00 – 115.00.**
Laurel Ladd Ciotti collection

Flamingo in gold-tone pot metal, with rhinestone wings, circa 1940. **$85.00 – 95.00.**
Laurel Ladd Ciotti collection

Unsigned flamingo in gold-tone pot metal, blue feather enameling, pink eye, circa 1940. **$95.00 – 110.00.** Author collection

Back view of flamingo.

Different style of flamingo pin, gold-tone with water ripples at his feet, blue stone over ½". Multicolored rhinestones across the bottom. Large stone is foiled and open in the back. **$75.00 – 95.00.** Author collection

Copy of famous Duchess of Windsor flamingo pin, with multicolored rhinestones, all stones are foiled and open in the back, 3½". **$40.00 – 55.00.** Author collection

Flamingo at Miami Beach, where else under the sun could the colors be so bright? Liberally covered with rhinestones, unsigned, 2". **$40.00 – 55.00.** Author collection

Napier Sterling atomic pearl pin from the 1950s, both words in block lettering. **$45.00 – 55.00.** Laurel Ladd Ciotti collection

Walter Lampl Sterling with 12 kt. rose gold–filled pin; stones may be glass or genuine aquamarines, circa 1944. **$135.00 – 155.00.** Laurel Ladd Ciotti collection

Coro Sterling Craft bow pin with rose gold vermeil and colored marquise rhinestones. **$85.00 – 90.00.** Laurel Ladd Ciotti collection

Retro bow pin with pale blue moonstones in plastic or Lucite, unmarked. **$50.00 – 60.00.** Laurel Ladd Ciotti collection

Unmarked bow pin with amethyst center stone, gold-tone. **$50.00 – 60.00.** Laurel Ladd Ciotti collection

Pearl and green stone floral spray, early 1940s, unmarked, 3". **$85.00 – 90.00.** Laurel Ladd Ciotti collection

Retro calla lilies pin with carnelian stones, unmarked. **$50.00 – 60.00.** Laurel Ladd Ciotti collection

KJL cross pin with yellow center stone, has a pendant bale. **$85.00 – 95.00.** Patti Collins Bultman collection

Gold-tone bow accented with green and red stone berries, and outlined in clear stones, unmarked. **$95.00 – 125.00.** Nancy Canãs collection

Boucher Deco style brooch with clear and blue rhinestones. **$65.00 – 85.00.** Nancy Canãs collection

Fanciful crown pin with chain dangles and accented with colored rhinestones, gold-tone, unmarked. **$100.00 – 125.00.** Nancy Canãs collection

Boucher American flag pin, marked "0157P," enameled. **$95.00 – 120.00.** Nancy Canãs collection

Napier eagle brooch with American flag pattern, gold-tone. **$75.00 – 85.00.** Nancy Canãs collection

Original by Robert bee pin, enameled in orange and black. **$55.00 – 70.00.** Nancy Canãs collection

Vendôme lion brooch, brushed silver-tone with a faux ivory body. **$125.00 – 150.00.** Nancy Canãs collection

ART poinsettia brooch, enameled, with green and red rhinestones. **$45.00 – 65.00.** Nancy Canãs collection

Chanel Lucite sun brooch, gold-tone sun is a raised design. **$350.00 – 450.00.** Nancy Canãs collection

Boucher grasshopper, gold-tone with green eyes, marked "0815P." **$75.00 – 120.00.** Nancy Canãs collection

Large flower brooch, japanned, unmarked. **$95.00 – 120.00.** Nancy Canãs collection

Kenneth Lane red cross-style brooch, red enameling and clear stones. **$60.00 – 85.00.** Nancy Canãs collection

KJL Bumblebee pin, enameled with green eyes. **$80.00 – 105.00.** Nancy Canãs collection

Kenneth Lane enameled frog with clear rhinestones, gold-tone. **$80.00 – 95.00.** Nancy Canãs collection

Kenneth Lane white enameled alligator pin with rhinestones on head, feet, and tail. **$120.00 – 140.00.** Nancy Canãs collection

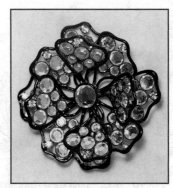

Kenneth Lane japanned brooch with clear rhine-stones. **$45.00 – 65.00.** Nancy Canãs collection

KJL green enameled monkey pin, wearing an earring, has a dangle on his arm, probably a piece of fruit. Big cabochon eyes. **$195.00 – 230.00.** Nancy Canãs collection

KERR watch fob marked "Sterling 173," circa 1900, an angel, great detailing. **$275.00 – 300.00.** Nancy Canás collection

Eisenberg brooch, signed "E" in script, dark purple rhinestones around center, clear stones finish pin. **$300.00 – 400.00.** Nancy Canás collection

Joseff Hollywood silver-tone brooch of three bees. **$350.00 – 450.00.** Nancy Canás collection

Pauline Rader ram brooch, purple and white enameling, green stone eye. **$125.00 – 145.00.** Nancy Canás collection

Sapphire and clear flowers in a sapphire vase, unmarked. **$110.00 – 135.00.** Nancy Canás collection

Cadoro brooch with an enormous glass amethyst center stone, 1¼", surrounded by pearls and rhinestones in a star motif. **$95.00 – 105.00.** Georgia Robinson collection

Cadoro snowflake brooch in gold-tone with pearls and topaz rhinestones. **$80.00 – 95.00.** Georgia Robinson collection

Weiss silver-tone spoke brooch, center stone is nearly 1", its faceted and blobby spokes are made of clear rhinestones. **$75.00 – 95.00.** Georgia Robinson collection

Coro stylized leaf spray with clear marquise stones; looks like the wind just blew across it. **$100.00 – 120.00.** Georgia Robinson collection

Coro retro floral bouquet with a ribbon, multicolored rhinestones. **$55.00 – 65.00.** Georgia Robinson collection

Miriam Haskell gold-tone bow with dangling locket, accented with coral glass beads and rhinestones, it is marked on the back of the bow and on the back of the locket, which opens. **$250.00 – 300.00.** Georgia Robinson collection

Back view of Miriam Haskell gold-tone bow with dangling locket.

CoroCraft gold-tone old-fashioned girl carrying a bouquet of flowers, accented with red, blue, and clear rhinestones, 2½". **$500.00 – 650.00.** Georgia Robinson collection

Castlecliff silver-tone brooch with Montana blue and clear rhinestones. **$95.00 – 115.00.** Georgia Robinson collection

Alice Caviness scarf pin, green and blue rhinestones on an oval design, gold-tone. **$65.00 – 80.00.** Georgia Robinson collection

Peacock fur clip, hand-soldered construction, unsigned, 4", one-of-a-kind. **$245.00 – 265.00.** Kim Paff collection

Unsigned but patent-verified Alfred Phillipe for Trifari French paste-style trembler, 2¼", with two tremblers. **$300.00 – 350.00.** Kim Paff collection

Rhinestone and enamel palm tree pin, 2½", possibly a Marie Petit design. **$225.00 – 240.00.** Kim Paff collection

Boucher brooch, signed and numbered 3089, clear and aqua stones, 2", gold- and silver-tone. **$175.00 – 205.00.** Kim Paff collection

Double fur clip, marked "Sterling," 3½" with rhinestones and rhinestone dangle. Rare. **$245.00 – 260.00.** Kim Paff collection

Original by Robert black glass cameo brooch/pendant, 2" with the signed palette. **$75.00 – 85.00.** Kim Paff collection

Unsigned blue trapezoid rhinestones and clear rhinestones brooch, silver on pot metal, 2¼". **$60.00 – 70.00.** Kim Paff collection.

C R Co. moth fur clip, 12kt. gold filled, double clip, pinch-open wings, clear, aqua, and red rhinestones. **$100.00 – 125.00.** Kim Paff collection

Trembler bug pin, art glass and rhinestones, upside down rivoli stones, unsigned Schreiner. **$150.00 – 165.00.** Kim Paff collection

Coro Sterling hand mirror pin, signed and attributed to Adolf Katz. **$275.00 – 395.00.** Kim Paff collection

Original by Robert floral brooch with filigree and multicolored rhinestones. **$75.00 – 95.00.** Kim Paff collection

Original by Robert pin with large purple cabochon center stone, pearls, gold-tone. **$60.00 – 70.00.** Kim Paff collection

Made in Austria leaf brooch with olivine and topaz stones. **$60.00 – $70.00.** Kim Paff collection

Leaf pin in aqua aurora borealis stones, unsigned. **$50.00 – 60.00.** Kim Paff collection

Miriam Haskell–style shell slice with pink quartz dangles and green quartz beads held in place by rhinestone-head pins. **$300.00 – 325.00.** Kim Paff collection

Original by Robert white stone and silver filigree pin. **$60.00 – 70.00.** Kim Paff collection

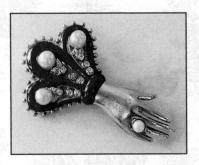

Red enamel hand pin with pearls, 2¼", unsigned. **$25.00 – 35.00.** Kim Paff collection

Hand pin holding flowers and leaves, enamel and rhinestones, 3½". **$50.00 – $70.00.** Kim Paff collection

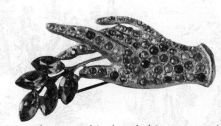

Hand pin, multicolored rhinestones with green marquise-shaped leaves, 2½", 1930s, bell-shaped mark on back, unknown. **$50.00 – 65.00.** Kim Paff collection

Mark on back of hand pin.

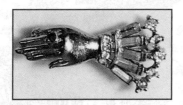

Tiny hand pin, only 1½", rhinestone cuff. **$30.00 – 40.00.** Kim Paff collection

HAR jester pin, enameled, part of a series. **$25.00 – 55.00.** Author collection

Coro fur clip, apparently used like a scatter pin, 1" only, with rhinestones and a tiny brushing of enamel around the center flower. Very sturdy and well made, ½". **$25.00 – 35.00.** Author collection

Spain signed Spanish galleon inside anchor pin, damascene. **$20.00 – 25.00.** Author collection

Egyptian-themed pin, damascene, unsigned, hollow. **$40.00 – 45.00.** Author collection

Spain signed Spanish string instrument with damascene neck. **$50.00 – 65.00.** Author collection

Sunflower pin ftom the 1970s, 2½", enameled. **$5.00 – 10.00.** Author collection

Orchid fur clip, pale and dark purple enameling with rhinestones. **$75.00 – 115.00.** Author collection

Yellow daisy flower pin with green leaves, enameled, almost 3". **$10.00 – 20.00.** Author collection

Psychedelic enameled butterfly from the 1970s, with blue stones on body, almost 3½". **$25.00 – 35.00.** Author collection

Seahorse with plastic body accented with pale lavender stones. **$25.00 – 40.00.** Author collection

Enamel and rhinestone seahorse pin. **$15.00 – 20.00.** Author collection

Pauline Rader trembler butterfly in silver-tone, green rhinestone eyes, 4". **$35.00 – 55.00.** Author collection

HAR enameled flower with rhinestone center. **$40.00 – 55.00.** Author collection

KJL spider in blues, available in other colors and by other companies. **$25.00 – 30.00.** Author collection

Kenneth Lane Humpty Dumpty pin, all dressed up, no one to fall for. **$95.00 – 125.00.** Author collection

Trifari seahorse pin with teal stone dangle, dated 1990, beautiful choice of stone colors and shapes. **$45.00 – 75.00.** Author collection

Cornucopia pin with clear and blue rhinestones, 3½", gold-tone pot metal. **$55.00 – 80.00.** Author collection

Monkey in a coconut tree, hanging on to a coconut. Enameling and rhinestones, 3", tree trunk is brown and green. I have seen this pin in a variety of enameled colors and rhinestones. Still a favorite. **$125.00 – 175.00.** Author collection

Back view of monkey pin.

Van S. Authentics stick pin with 1" wide center stone, foiled and open backed, safety chain. Rare. **$100.00 – 125.00.** Author collection

This pin was purchased sixteen years ago from a Florida store called Maas Bros. It came on a card I carelessly threw away, one year before I began collecting vintage costume jewelry. It looks like platinum, diamonds, and a ruby, 2½". **$25.00 – 60.00.** Author collection

Weiss snake pin with fangs in heliotrope rhinestones, with pink eyes, 5". I have seen this pin marked "KJL," "Parklane," and "Capri." Tail is finished with two pear-shaped stones. Viewed from the side, he has a bottom lip, with rhinestones under the fangs. I wear him everywhere but church. **$130.00 – 150.00.** Author collection

Lovebirds on a branch; birds have coral cabochons, green stone eyes, and their branch is accented with stones, 2". **$25.00 – 40.00.** Author collection

This little fish with the purple belly and lavender stone eye is very well made, almost 1½". **$65.00 – 75.00.** Author collection

Back view of purple-bellied fish pin.

Unmarked Panetta fish pin, enameled with rhinestones, over 2½". **$120.00 – 145.00.** Author collection

This massive green rhinestone pin has a 1⅜" clear glass unfoiled center stone; all stones are prong set. **$80.00 – 95.00.** Author collection

Coro Pegasus bird pin in gold-tone, with red eyes, 2½". **$95.00 – 120.00.** Author collection

Weinberg New York bar pin with invisibly set green stones surrounded by clears, 2½". Weinberg is famous for its invisibly set stones. **$75.00 – 95.00.** Author collection

Enameled palm trees pin with clear rhinestones, 1¾". **$20.00 – 25.00.** Author collection

Gerry's white shell crab pin with rhinestone accents, 1¼". **$10.00 – 20.00.** Author collection

Punchy, the Hawaiian Punch guy; how'd you like a nice Hawaiian punch? Enameled, 1¼", with a dinged nose and toe. Crossover collectible. **$60.00 – 75.00.** Author collection

Coro pearl fish pin with green eye, 2½". **$80.00 – 95.00.** Author collection

An amazing piece of runway jewelry, this star is over 4"; the topaz center stone is 1". Runway jewelry consists of one-of-a-kind pieces that were made to be worn on the fashion runway; they usually have bold, over-the-top designs, and are easily seen from a distance. Many are very well made and able to stand up to any wear; others were quickly made to accessorize an outfit and may not hold up to casual wear. **$125.00 – 150.00.** Author collection

Another "star" from my runway jewelry collection, this star pin has the biggest rhinestones I have ever seen in a piece of jewelry; the clear pear-shaped stones are almost 2". The star is almost 4½"; this piece is very well made, but very heavy; it would have to be attached to an undergarment or to outer wear such as a coat. **$150.00 – 180.00.** Author collection

Pauline Rader Victorian-style green stones and pearls brooch, 2¼", with a bale for a pendant. **$70.00 – 90.00.** Author collection

Back view of Rader pin with mark.

Adele Simpson star brooch with pearls and rhinestones, 2½". **$125.00 – 145.00.** Author collection

Eisenberg spray pin with clear rhinestones, 2⅜". **$45.00 – 65.00.** Author collection

Pansy pin, enameled, with a pearl center. **$20.00 – 35.00.** Author collection

Snowflake starburst pin in clear rhinestones with a pendant bale, 1½". **$25.00 – 40.00.** Author collection

Basket of flowers pin from the 1930s, half pearls, pink and blue stones and black enamel detailing, 2". This pin i marked with "NE" inside a wine glass. **$85.00 – 105.00.** Author collection

Back of NE in wine-glass basket pin.

I'm still trying to figure this one out. It is a massive sitting ballerina, almost 5" x 3½", with rhinestones inside the tutu folds, a very expressive and graceful pin. Some type of hammered silver metal, probably hand crafted for a specific event. Weighs over 1lb. **$70.00 – 95.00.** Author collection

Mimi di N gold-tone elephant, part of a series from the 1970s through the early 1990s, this one is dated "1987," almost 3". Mimi di N is Mimi di Nascemi, a designer who started business in 1962; her jewelry is eye catching, large scale, and dramatic, as seen by this elephant brooch. Many collectors think her jewelry is signed "Mimi din," and therefore, it can be purchased sometimes for bargain prices. **$150.00 – 165.00.** Author collection

Mimi di N tiger pin, over 3", signed and dated "1993." **$150.00 – 165.00.** Author collection

Mimi di N frog pendant and clip earrings; pendant is marked "Mimi di N" and "1973," earrings are signed on a plaque inside the back of the frog and on the earring clip. **$165.00 – 195.00.** Author collection

Bird in flight pin, champagne rhinestones, 2½", gold wash. **$55.00 – 70.00.** Author collection

Craft scorpion enameled pin with green eyes, accented with clear stones, 2"; I wear this sometimes to warn others of my mood. **$50.00 – 65.00.** Author collection

Brania butterfly pin in topaz and aurora borealis clear stones, japanned, 2½". **$135.00 – 165.00.** Author collection

Van Dell floral spray brooch in original paper and fabric box, tag inside says "Precious·All trademark ½₀-12k GF on Sterling," pin is marked "Van Dell ½₀ 12k gf Sterling," gold wash is yellow gold and rose gold, leaves and stem are yellow, flowers and ribbon are rose, purple rhinestones, 5½". **$125.00 – 140.00.** Author collection

Peridot and clear rhinestones on a stylized floral pin, 2½", all peridot green stones are open in the back. **$70.00 – 85.00.** Author collection

Van Dell floral spray brooch. A pin is a pin, but a big ol' pin is a brooch.

Japanned floral spray with olivine and orange stones, 3". **$25.00 – 45.00.** Author collection

JJ toucan pin, enameled, 1¾"; these pins have a big following, they are whimsical and fun, with almost limitless designs. **$35.00 – 45.00.** Author collection

Pakula pin in original box, tag reads "Cultured Pearl by Pakula," 2". **$25.00 – 35.00.** Author collection

Topaz chatelaine, glass center stones are open in the back, chain is 4½". **$25.00 – 45.00.** Author collection

Elephant and mahout chatelaine circa 1930s, brass wash pot metal, chain is over 5", elephant is over 2". A mahout is an elephant handler. **$120.00 – 145.00.** Author collection

Jeanne bird with bird nest and eggs, nest is hand wired. **$50.00 – 65.00.** Author collection

White plastic Christmas tree pin with pink pearls and glitter. This pin belonged to my grandmother, Marie Poremba Mitchell, and I look forward to owning it. As a family heirloom it is priceless, but examples can be found for **$15.00 – 20.00.** Blanche Gladis Poremba collection

Earrings

Original by Robert black and gold dangle earrings. **$60.00 – 70.00.** Kim Paff collection

Unsigned hand-wired pearl ear wraps, gold-tone with faux pearls, worn around the ear. **$95.00 – 115.00.** Kim Paff collection

Black glass and gold leaf earrings with clear rhinestones, 1¼". **$30.00 – 35.00.** Kim Paff collection

Vendôme green cabochon earrings. **$45.00 – 65.00.** Georgia Robinson collection

Miriam Haskell gold-tone clip earrings, large marbled green cabochon stone accented with genuine coral beads and glass coral seed beads, with wired rhinestones. **$125.00 – 160.00.** Georgia Robinson collection

Back view of Miriam Haskell green earring.

Miriam Haskell turquoise glass earrings, with rhinestone accents and a large turquoise bead inside the flower bud. **$95.00 – 105.00.** Georgia Robinson collection

Back view of Miriam Haskell turquoise earring.

Schiaparelli earrings, pale blue large stones, gold-plated. **$55.00 – 70.00.** Nancy Canãs collection

Chanel clip earrings, Lucite with embedded "CC," the Chanel trademark. **$175.00 – 250.00.** Nancy Canãs collection

Flag earrings in red, clear, and blue rhinestones, unsigned. **$40.00 – 45.00.** Nancy Canãs collection

Kenneth Lane clip earrings, two pairs, bug designs in gold-tone. **$45.00 – 50.00** per pair. Nancy Canãs collection

KJL large blue cabochon earrings with red cabochons and pavéd clear stones. **$85.00 – 95.00.** Nancy Canãs collection

Trifari clear baguette rhinestone earrings, **$65.00 – 75.00.** Nancy Canãs collection

Austria shades of blue and green earrings, marked "Austria" on bottom of ear clasp. **$45.00 – 50.00.** Patti Collins Bultman collection

Black dangle earrings, plastic stone and clear rhinestones. **$45.00 – 50.00.** Patti Collins Bultman collection

Austria earrings in topaz and aurora borealis mix of stones, marked on back of base behind clip. **$45.00 – 50.00.** Patti Collins Bultman collection

Miriam Haskell olive faceted tube beads with paprika art glass beads; pierced earrings are signed on back, 2½". **$110.00 – 125.00.** Patti Collins Bultman collection

Miriam Haskell swirled brown and white art glass bead pierced earrings, with faceted tube beads, signed on back of earrings around post. **$85.00 – 95.00.** Patti Collins Bultman collection

Back of Miriam Haskell earrings.

Alice Caviness art glass earrings in shades of pink. **$35.00 – 45.00.** Author collection

Alice Caviness art glass earrings in teal.
$45.00 – 50.00. Author collection

Craft earrings with pastel rhinestones and pearls, the pearls are enclosed in a grid work basket and move around freely, rim of earrings is enameled around the stones, very heavy, over 1½". **$45.00 – 60.00.** Author collection

Green marquise rhine-stone earrings. **$20.00 – 25.00.** Author collection

Beau Jewels blue stone earrings in silver-tone, 1½". **$35.00 – 45.00.** Author collection

ART earrings with green glass cabochons and pearls, gold-tone with silver-tone accents and clear rhinestones, 1¼"; only one ear-ring is marked. **$45.00 – 55.00.** Author collection

Back of ART earring.

Vogue crystal bead earrings, wire wrapped, with clear rhinestones, clip on. **$30.00 – 40.00.** Author collection

Unsigned emerald green and peridot square earrings, ¾". **$25.00 – 30.00.** Author collection

The signature was placed on these under the ear clip and is almost impossible to read; you really have to know it says "Jesara," in script, to be able to recognize the mark. The design is similar to the earrings that go with the Trifari crown pins. Stones are both plastic. **$20.00 – 25.00.** Author collection

Classic-style earrings, with faceted red glass center stones and channel-set rhinestones. **$30.00 – 35.00.** Author collection

Mimi di N white button earrings, signed and dated "1978." **$35.00 – 50.00.** Author collection

Mimi di N earrings with faux pearls and rhinestone rondelles. **$45.00 – 65.00.** Author collection

Kramer topaz earrings, antique gold finish. **$20.00 – 25.00.** Author collection

Ann Vien green earrings, on original card, with a big green cabochon filled with silver flecks; all stones are prong set. Rare. **$65.00 – 90.00.** Author collection

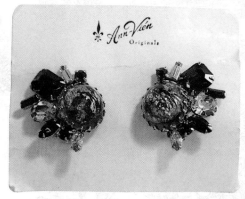

Back view of Ann Vien earrings with signature.

Ann Vien pearl earrings, 2". Rare. **$30.00 – 40.00.** Author collection

Unsigned earrings in smoky rhinestones. **$10.00 – 15.00.** Author collection

Pink chandelier earrings, probably unsigned Hattie Carnegie; the style and design are identical. **$25.00 – 30.00.** Author collection

Hollycraft topaz flower earrings, marked "Hollycraft COPR 1954" on back of earring itself, and "Hollycraft" on back of clip. **$40.00 – 45.00.** Author collection

These green glass earrings are a classic design, unsigned; notice the way the stones are set. **$25.00 – 30.00.** Author collection

Kenneth Lane white plastic bead earrings. **$20.00 – 30.00.** Author collection

Tortolani red cabochon and pearl earrings, gold-tone, built-in plastic comfort pad, stones are open in the back. **$25.00 – 45.00.** Author collection

Miriam Haskell earrings with rhinestones and white pearls. **$55.00 – 70.00.** Author collection

Back view of Miriam Haskell earring.

These unmarked earrings look like Haskell; pearls and rhinestones. **$25.00 – 30.00.** Author collection

The seed pearls that surround this pearl button are hand strung. Unsigned. **$5.00 – 10.00.** Author collection

Rings & Things

Black Lucite ring with clear rhinestones. **$45.00 – 55.00.**
Nancy Canãs collection

KJL rings, large cushion-cut crystal stones in gold-tone mounting. **$55.00 – 90.00.**
Nancy Canãs collection

Kenneth Lane ring, adjustable gold mesh wrap ring with a panther with red stone eyes and clear stone accents. **$85.00 – 125.00.**
Nancy Canãs collection

Continental ruby red bug hair clip, body is a carved, frosted red glass stone, prong set, wings are finished with a tiny pink stone. Continental is a Canadian company. **$45.00 – 55.00.** Author collection

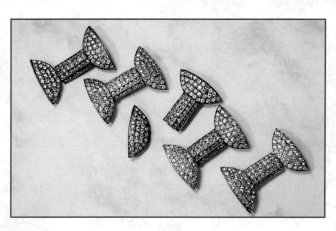

Unsigned "frogs" rhinestone set, 1½" long, these two-piece frog clasps were made to be sewn on clothes, one shown unfastened, silver-plated pot metal. **$25.00 – 50.00** set. Kim Paff collection

Open view of box.

Brania trinket box has gold-flecked cabochon stones, blue glass beads, and a carved brown glass center stone; outlined with rhinestone chain, signed inside box, and has a hang tag. **$165.00 – 190.00.** Author collection

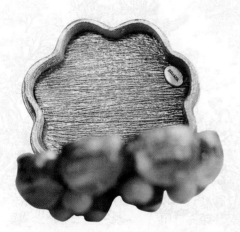

Inside view of box with Brania signature.

Brania hang tag.

Original by Robert ring with enormous center stone with an opal-like array of colors. This ring is adjustable to any size finger, due to the design of the shank. Rare. **$55.00 – 75.00.** Author collection

Close-up view of back of ring with signature.

Pebble Jewelry

Pebble jewelry is made by Miracle Jewelry Company, Mizpah Jewelry Company, and Exquisite Jewelry Company.

Miracle thistle silver-tone pin with large unfoiled purple stones. **$50.00 – 60.00.** Laurel Ladd Ciotti collection

Miracle thistle pin, silver-tone with three malachite stones. **$45.00 – 50.00.** Laurel Ladd Ciotti collection

Pair of Irish hearts pins with simulated Connemara marble. **$45.00 – 50.00** pair. Laurel Ladd Ciotti collection

Agate pin, gold-tone. **$50.00 – 55.00.** Laurel Ladd Ciotti collection

Miracle pennular brooch, simulates a cloak clasp; notice the different colored stones. **$50.00 – 55.00.** Laurel Ladd Ciotti collection

Miracle pebble bracelet, adjustable with stone dangle, has a variety of stones. **$65.00 – 75.00.** Laurel Ladd Ciotti collection

Miracle thistles with marcasites and simulated cairngorm (special color — goldish/orangeish) stones. **$55.00 – 60.00.** Laurel Ladd Ciotti collection

Miracle glass cairngorm earrings. **$30.00 – 35.00.** Laurel Ladd Ciotti collection

Miracle pebble pin, probably glass agate. **$50.00 – 55.00.** Laurel Ladd Ciotti collection

Miracle round pin with brown stones, simulated cairngorm. **$50.00 – 55.00.** Laurel Ladd Ciotti collection

Unsigned bagpipes, plaid enamel, C clasp. **$50.00 – 60.00.** Laurel Ladd Ciotti collection

Miracle thistle ring. **$35.00 – 40.00.** Laurel Ladd Ciotti collection

Exquisite kilt pin, round amethyst stone, oval blue stone, and black and white triangle stone. Exquisite is a Canadian British company. **$50.00 – 55.00.** Laurel Ladd Ciotti collection

Mizpah kilt pin or dagger, over 3" long with amethyst stones. **$50.00 – 55.00.** Laurel Ladd Ciotti collection

Guilloche

Goldette reverse-painted glass bracelet from the 1950s, center is green. **$90.00 – 110.00.** Laurel Ladd Ciotti collection

Locket pendant, typical rose motif. **$75.00 – 95.00.** Laurel Ladd Ciotti collection

This is a four-picture locket with pink roses and pearls on fleur-de-lis holder, pictured in an ad from 1950. **$125.00 – 150.00.** Laurel Ladd Ciotti collection

Four-picture locket opened to show four photos.

Reverse-painted black heart pin with clear rhinestones, 1950s. **$40.00 – 50.00.** Laurel Ladd Ciotti collection

Brass and glass brooch with twisted rope border. **$45.00 – 55.00.** Laurel Ladd Ciotti collection

Elgin America hand-painted rose pin, has original label still on back of pin. **$65.00 – 75.00.** Laurel Ladd Ciotti collection

Back view showing Elgin America label.

Brooch with a Devonshire Cream guilloche, hand painted. **$70.00 – 90.00.** Laurel Ladd Ciotti collection

Brass pin with filigree, hand painted, circa 1950. **$60.00 – 70.00.** Laurel Ladd Ciotti collection

Pendant with typical rose motif, rhinestone trim, and a tassel. **$50.00 – 65.00.** Laurel Ladd Ciotti collection

Hidden picture brooch holds two photos. Hand painted. Shown are one brooch open and one brooch closed. **$95.00 – 120.00.** Laurel Ladd Ciotti collection

Contemporary Jewelry

Each time I go to a department store, I make sure to wander through the contemporary costume jewelry department. I love to see what is new, and compare it with the old. It is a chance to see the names and work of new designers. And I ALWAYS check out the sale racks for bargains. And have you seen the new Swarovski line of jewelry? It is quite amazing and well made, and I believe it will be highly desired in the future.

Many of the collectors I know disdain the new costume jewelry. But the vintage costume jewelry we all covet was new in the department store at one time. We could be buying the desired costume jewelry of the future, and our daughters and granddaughters will surely thank us for it.

Checking out the contemporary jewelry is a great way for new collectors to recognize the new styles and current manufacturing techniques. New jewelry ends up in showcases at antique shops and malls, and you need to know who is making what, and maybe avoid paying vintage prices for new jewelry.

I have a large collection of contemporary jewelry, and I am as proud to wear it as I am some of my oldest jewels. I hope you enjoy the coming attractions, and make it a point to go yourself and have a look.

Ann Klein snake chain necklace with thick Lucite cross flecked with gold. **$50.00 – 65.00.** Nancy Canãs collection

L'Officiel Made in Italy massive daisy bouquet with clear and amber stones and carved green glass leaves, 5¼ ". **$300.00 – 350.00.** Georgia Robinson collection

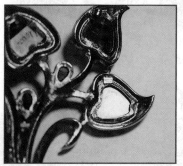

L'Officiel Made in Italy flower brooch with fantasy tulip-like flowers or flower buds, 3½ ". **$275.00 – 300.00.** Georgia Robinson collection

Lavender enameled shrimp with red eyes and clear rhinestones. **$15.00 – 20.00.** Laurel Ladd Ciotti collection

Spike, the little bird, is a lapel pin; he has a clear rhinestone eye, and cute little birdie feet. **$5.00 – 10.00.** Author collection

Parrot on rhinestone swing, multi-colored prong-set stones, tail feathers are on a rhinestone chain and move freely, 6¼". **$50.00 – 65.00.** Authors collection

Hand-beaded parure made by Annie Navetta, using vintage jewelry, vintage components, and beads. Annie's talent is obvious in these designs she hand crafted; her jewelry is signed with a gold-tone metal tag that says "Anni." Many of her designs are built around vintage costume jewelry pins; she custom designs these for her customers without damaging the original vintage piece. Earrings, **$30.00 – 35.00.** Pin, **$70.00 – 80.00.** Necklace, **$150.00 – 165.00.** Author collection

Close-up of necklace.

Close-up of brooch.

Close-up of earrings.

Annie Navetta stretch bracelet absolutely covered with vintage glass beads, many combined to look like flowers. Pin, **$195.00 – 200.00.** Author collection

Donald Richards by don-lin articulated cowboy outfit with guns, all gold-tone except for silver-tone boots with spurs. It has lots of movement and noise, and is great fun to wear, especially now that I am a Texan. **$50.00 – 75.00.** Author collection

Annie Navetta fruit necklace, another one of Annie's stunning original designs. **$95.00 – 105.00.** Author collection

Matching fruit bracelet. **$65.00 – 75.00.**

Matching fruit earrings. **$22.00 – 27.00.**

Liz Claiborne bracelet with pale and dark blue rhinestones. Most of her jewelry is signed with a script "LC." **$25.00 – 40.00.** Author collection

Miriam Haskell stretch bracelet in shades of purple. **$25.00 – 40.00.** Author collection

Miriam Haskell floral stretch bracelet with tiny rhinestones. **$25.00 – 40.00.** Author collection

Miriam Haskell stretch bracelet with a regal look. These bracelets are not signed; they have only the price tag with the signature on it. **$25.00 – 40.00.** Author collection

Bijoux Cascio carousel horse head pin in original box, 2½", enamel and rhinestones. **$50.00 – 70.00.** Author collection

Suzanne Bjøntegård is a clothing designer who branched out a little into jewelry design. Her fruit jewelry is my favorite; this pear pin in its original box with its original tags is 2" long. Some of the boxes have care tags enclosed. Her jewelry is all signed, except for the small pieces, which have her initials. It is made in England. **$40.00 – 65.00.** Author collection

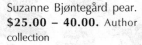

Suzanne Bjøntegård pear. **$25.00 – 40.00.** Author collection

Back of pear with signature.

Suzanne Bjøntegård pineapple pin with original tag. **$25.00 – 40.00.** Author collection

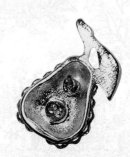

Back of pineapple pin with initials "SB." Author collection

Bright pink rhinestone pig with green stone eyes. **$20.00 – 25.00.** Author collection

Suzanne Bjøntegård apple pin. **$30.00 – 50.00.** Author collection

My kind of Christmas tree pin, BIG. It is 3¼". My collection of Christmas tree pins numbers over 300. **$55.00 – 75.00.** Author collection

Another fun, big tree pin; it has its own ornaments dangling from it, 4¼". **$55.00 – 75.00.** Author collection

Have you seen the wonderful five-inch long snake pins? They are being made in every color scheme and with a multitude of manufacturer's names on the back. Deco pot metal jewelry is also abundant in the secondary market.

What can we learn about these reproductions to make us smarter buyers? Worth repeating is the fact of knowing your dealer. Check out books, especially older jewelry books from the library to learn about the jewelry that is now being re-done. Build your own library of jewelry books. Attend any shows you can, look at all the booths and ask questions of the dealers. Most are willing to chat and share information, especially to a new collector. Cultivate friendships with older ladies who bought the jewelry new, and can tell you where they bought it, and sometimes how much they paid for it. Look through old magazines at the ads featuring jewelry; November and December issues are the best as they featured jewelry for Christmas gifts. And whenever you see someone wearing a lovely vintage brooch or bracelet, compliment them on it. You never know where it might lead.

This Staret Torch is over 4" tall, with glued and prong- set stones. It is a beautiful piece of jewelry. I have taken it and compared it with Staret jewelry in other people's collections, and those few pieces found in antique shops and malls. I know that the design is slightly different from the original design. Ripley's once sold a Staret Torch at auction for **$1,600.00.**

There are new copies of the Staret Torch being made, but they are easily recognized as new; one version is shiny gold-tone, completely different.

Back view of Staret Torch.

Column #2:

In November, a Trifari water bird came up for auction on the Internet, and before it ended at over eleven hundred dollars, it had caused a slight uproar in the online costume jewelry world. Why? Because an original Trifari Stork pin had recently sold at a Doyle auction in New York City for three thousand dollars, amongst furious bidding, and the Trifari water bird on the Internet auction was a . . . reproduction of the famous Trifari Stork, although a vintage reproduction. It is commonly called a stork, though it appears to be a heron.

During the course of the discussions, I ran across a collector/dealer named Deborah Kosnett, owner of www.rhinestonerainbow.com, who provides a section of fakes and reproductions on her website. This section frankly discusses in depth some of the more well-known fakes and reproductions, along with characteristics to educate the reader. I would like to introduce you to Deborah Kosnett, give you some of her background, and talk about the need for fakes pages such as hers. The following is a synopsis of my email interview with her.

Kosnett had always liked jewelry, but was not a collector. Then two things happened to change that; she viewed the Jewels of Fantasy at a nearby museum, and discovered beading.

Next according to Kosnett, "on a snowy weekend in February, 1997, I stumbled across eBay, then known as AuctionWeb. At first, I looked up bead auctions, but gradually I became fascinated by the pieces of costume jewelry that I kept seeing. I bid on and won a few, and started a costume jewelry collection." Kosnett continues, "A couple of months after I started cruising eBay, I discovered Jewelcollect. I joined and almost immediately became deeply involved with costume jewelry (became immersed in it would be a better description.)"

"I decided to set up a simple web site to display my beaded items, as well as vintage costume jewelry. The vintage jewelry ended up taking over, and today vintage jewelry is pretty much the only thing I deal in" says Kosnett. "I am a registered member of Jewelcollect, as well as a member of the Vintage, Fashion and Costume Jewelry (VFCJ) Club, and am a confirmed costume jewelry 'addict,'" she admits.

So how did she get from being a collector/dealer to educating fellow collectors? It all began at a VFCJ mini-convention, where members and collectors meet in various locations around the country to show, tell, sell and learn. Says Kosnett; "one of the speakers was Carole Ann Ashley, a fakes expert who has written several articles on the subject. As a result of her talk, not only did I learn that a Trifari turtle that I had recently purchased was not genuine, I got an idea of just how commonplace fakes can be in the costume jewelry world. I had, of course, heard of fakes in the high-end antiques world, but until then I had not thought that such existed in the world of costume jewelry.

"The idea of costume jewelry fakes fascinated me, and I wanted to learn more — not only to protect my own pocketbook, but also to avoid unknowingly selling fakes to my customers," states Kosnett. "I actually set up my first fakes pages about two years ago, when I ran across an online auction of the sought-after Coro Craft 'fighting fish.' Being the owner of a genuine Coro Craft fish, I noticed that the fish being offered at auction did not look like my fish, and in fact looked very much like the fake fish Carole had displayed in her lecture. . . . On a whim, I decided to set up an online side-by-side comparison page that would allow potential customers to learn the difference between the real and the fake. The fish page led to more pages. . . . I also have become an active collector of fakes."

I asked Kosnett to tell me why it is important for collectors, new and old, to be aware of fakes and repros. "That's easy: money," she declared. "If you unknowingly buy a fake, you're not getting what you paid for. . . . If you buy the fake, thinking you're buying the real thing, you are wasting your money. And, if you're buying a piece for investment purposes (something which I never recommend, by the way), if it's not genuine, your investment is worth less than you thought it was."

Kosnett continues, "Fakes are a fraud, pure and simple. They are a deliberate misrepresentation of a genuine item. Anyone who knowingly sells a fake without representing it for what it really is, is cheating the customer.

Through my fakes pages, I'm doing what I can to combat this, and to promote honesty in the vintage costume jewelry business."

I wondered if we should be worried about everything in our jewelry boxes, but Kosnett put this worry to rest, saying, "Generally speaking, you're likely to find fakes only of high-end pieces. Why? Because who would bother faking a low-end piece? It wouldn't be economically feasible, because a low-end piece will not bring a lot of money in the vintage market." On another interesting note, Kosnett tells us "some fakes are not copies of genuine pieces, but are entirely made-up designs. This is especially true of jelly bellies, where some jellies labeled 'Trifari' and 'Hobé' have no genuine counterparts, and in fact are poorly and cheaply made. . . . Hobé never made jellies."

Kosnett features eight items, all brooches, on her fakes pages. The first is the Boucher enameled Grasshopper pin, Kosnett shows a real and two fake pins. Her detailed information and close-up photos tell readers how to tell the difference. The genuine grasshopper is one and one-half inches by three and seven-eighths inches, with a silver head. The two fakes are three and one-half inches long, and the coloring and head shapes differ from the genuine.

Next is the Coro Craft Fighting Fish that first got her attention. This wide-mouth fish, with a large rhinestone mouth, has smooth closed-loop fins, while the fake has bumpy open-loop fins. Then comes the Eisenberg Char Woman; the real one is a fur clip, but the fake has a pin back and is poorly made and cheap looking.

The Staret Torch pin is a beauty, with a lady's hand holding a lit torch aloft. The genuine pin has a shorter, fatter flame, a double row of rhinestones on the sleeve and red stones. The fake has a long fingernail on the thumb that shows and a single row of rhinestones on the sleeve.

The last three pages highlight Trifari pins; two jelly bellies and the Stork pin. Kosnett states the real jelly belly peony is easy to identify; its petals have real molded indentations, which are deep and sharply curved. The fake is shallower and narrower, and doesn't curve much; in addition, the back is poorly finished. The real jelly belly crab is also easy to identify; the jelly belly body is crab shaped, where the fake is round.

Kosnett's pages of the Trifari Stork pin show five versions of the stork, all very similar, with two real ones, one possible, and two fakes. Each is so similar it is very hard to determine differences. Kosnett however, offers a copy of the original design patent, which shows the design to have a fur clip, not a pin back.

It is important to note that these copies or reproductions also fall into the vintage category. Most were knocked off at the time the genuine piece was available. The practice of making knockoffs exists even today, in the clothing, jewelry and accessories fields.

Kosnett plans to add to her fakes pages very soon. She concludes, "With that in mind, does anybody out there have a Chanel enameled frog they'd like to sell me for under $75.00??? I'll even take the fake one (yes, I have it on good authority that the Chanel frog has been faked)."

Fakes & Reproductions

Column #3:

Reproductions and fakes are currently rampant in the world of vintage costume jewelry collecting. Fakes and reproductions affect all collectors and the value of their collections, whether extensive or small enough to fit in one jewelry box.

Weiss is the first on our list. The Weiss Company was founded in 1942 and remained in business through the early 1970s. There is an amazing glut of jewelry marked Weiss on the secondary market. Many are exact copies of genuine Weiss designs, but the color combinations of the rhinestones don't match the originals.

Another giveaway is seeing twenty or thirty of the same piece up for auction at one time. Unknowing or unscrupulous sellers apparently sit in front of their computers listing one item right after another right after another. They wouldn't be so obvious if they were spaced further apart. However, a collector doing a search for Weiss only would immediately pull up identical listings and should be able to recognize the duplicity.

Eisenberg is always ripe for reproductions. Beware of misleading descriptions that never actually state a piece is an Eisenberg.

Because of the high prices some examples of genuine Bakelite command, this field is frightfully flooded with fakes, known to collectors, thanks to Karima Parry, author of multiple books on Bakelite and owner of Plastic Fantastic, www.plasticfantastic.com, as "Fakelite." These pieces are coming from Taiwan in enormous quantities, in the most desired polka dots, bow ties, figurals, carved designs, even poker chip caddies.

Like fakes and reproductions in all collecting fields, it is not always the first buyers and sellers who suffer. Many honest sellers offer these items at very reasonable prices to collectors who can't or won't pay huge prices for the originals. These collectors like the designs and the dealers clearly state that these are copies or reproductions, and prices are low and reasonable. But sold two or three times, for increasing amounts each time, with neither buyer nor seller aware many times of the item's origins, and unsuspecting collectors, usually but not always novice collectors, pay hundreds of dollars for an item worth $25.00 or $30.00. There are also, unfortunately, dealers who believe in the "perceived value" rule — if they price these items high from the beginning, someone somewhere will believe these items are worth the price, and will part with the money. Sadly, they believe they are buying from an otherwise totally scrupulous dealer.

What can you do to protect yourself? Education is part of the answer; being honest with yourself is the other part. If you know what the original items looked like, by studying books and talking with trusted dealers and fellow collectors, you will know when these items appear "wrong." If you go to a show or into an antique shop, and the dealers are offering multiples of what you know is a truly rare piece, buyer beware. Is it statistically possible for a dealer to have 15 black and cream polka dot Bakelite bracelets? Not really. There ARE dealers who specialize in Bakelite and they may have a variety of great pieces but probably won't have multiples of the same design. And if you know the correct colors and carvings of the original Bakelite, you'll be able to spot instantly a piece of Taiwan "Fakelite."

The other part of the equation is being honest with yourself; if it seems too good to be true, then it probably is. If you are at a garage sale and a sweet little old man or lady has a shoebox of costume jewelry with one fantastic piece of Bakelite, you could have hit the jackpot. But if that same little old lady or man is set up at a big show and has boxes and boxes of the stuff, it is time for a reality check. Know your collectible and it won't bite you in the back.

F.Y.I. Hobé Cie Jewelry Company is still in business, and their current line can be found in many department stores. Check out the offerings the next time you are at the mall to familiarize yourself with it before purchasing Hobé secondhand or online.

Care & Repair

Many of the pieces that you buy will be 40 or 50 years old, maybe even older. They need a little bit of special handling to keep them happy and ready to wear.

First, never throw pieces in a box or drawer on top of one another. Pieces can become scratched or broken, and stones can be knocked out. Remember, this jewelry was meant to be disposable, designed for a specific season or outfit, and discarded when the next new thing came along. Fortunately for us, many of those manufacturers took great pride in their jewelry, and made it to last a lifetime. Or two.

It makes sense to buy the best quality you can afford, especially when buying rhinestone jewelry. Prong set is best, but even glued-in stones can have a long life with proper care.

Always put your jewelry on last, after you have applied hairspray and perfume. These products can dull the finish of rhinestones, even react with the glues and cause stones to pop out.

If you have a humidity problem where you live, take care to keep your jewelry free from the effects by adding silica packets, like those found in new handbags and shoes, liberally throughout the drawers holding your collection. Some collectors I know ask clerks at shoe stores to save these packets for them; other collectors buy enough shoes to create their own stockpile.

Celluloid needs to breathe; don't nestle it in cotton and put it in a box with a lid on it. Don't put a bunch of Celluloid all together. Most important, keep it well away from any heat source.

Don't be afraid to buy broken pieces of jewelry for the stones, if the price is right. Replacing missing or damaged stones is easier than you might think; it just takes patience and a steady hand. B'sue's Boutique sells a prong lifter tool in the event you have a lot of stones to replace. It is quite affordable and easy to use.

B'sue's Boutique, MRstones, and Jan's Jewels all sell mixed bags of loose rhinestones. MRstones sells repair kits that have a variety of stones in different colors and sizes. They offer tools and glue. I recommend G-S Hypo-Tube Cement. Don't use superglue; it may hold forever, but it may also cloud the stone. Experiment with G-S Hypo-Tube Cement to find the right amount; too little and the stone will fall back out, too much and you will be scraping dried glue off of your jewelry.

You don't need a lot of fancy tools in your jewelry repair kit. A pair of tweezers, an eyeglass kit of screwdrivers and two pairs of needle-nose pliers should get you started. Add some toothpicks and a large blunt sewing needle, and some Hypocement. These should cover the basics.

Toothpicks are perfect for positioning stones into their cups once you have put some glue into the cup. I've never been proficient at using tweezers for placing small stones; my old-fashioned way involves a wet finger lightly tapped on the top of the stone to move it into position. Larger stones can easily be picked up and moved into position with fingers or tweezers.

Restringing experts get $1.50 or $2.00 per knot for restringing pearls and beads. Here's my trade secret for you, anyone with patience can do it. It takes a lot of practice in the beginning to get the knots just right, but if you practice with an old strand of plastic beads, it is a talent you can master.

Many companies sell bead and string components; my favorite is Fire Mountain Gems. Their catalog lists the different stringing materials and tells you the appropriate use. They sell small and large quantities of these stringing materials. They also offer a variety of cups and caps to seal both ends of your necklaces and bracelets.

Bead cups that look like an oyster are the easiest to use. You simply tie a knot into the end of the string, slide the knot into the bead cup and squeeze it closed. You're ready to start restringing. Everyone has a method that works best for them. I slide a bead on the string down to the cup, make a large loose knot close to the bead, and use my blunt needle to maneuver the knot down to the bead. Slide the next bead down to the knot and pull snugly against the knot, causing it to tighten. Do not make your knots too tight, the necklace will buckle and refuse to lie flat when you wear it. Experience will allow you to become proficient at stringing. Don't be afraid to take it apart and redo it, as many times as necessary.

You may want to consider buying a bead board. These are flocked plastic boards with grooves for the beads to lie in, and lengths are marked off in inches. This aids in your design, or keeps the necklace in its original order, and keeps the beads from sliding all over the work surface. Bead boards are less than $10.00 and are well worth the money, if you plan on doing a lot of restringing.

The most important things to remember when attempting your own repairs is use a gentle touch. Practice lifting and replacing prongs on a broken piece of jewelry before attempting to repair a good piece.

When resetting stones, I try to do several at one time. The first few times you open G-S Hypo-Tube Cement, it seems to gush out of the tube. I keep a plastic or paper plate handy, dab the glue onto the plate, replace the cap on the glue then use toothpicks to put spots of glue into the stone cups. G-S Hypo-Tube Cement dries quickly and the jewelry should sit overnight before wearing. I usually place the glued jewelry in a box with a lid to keep it from being moved or bumped while drying. The next day I take the piece of jewelry, hold it over white paper or a paper towel, and tap it firmly to make sure the stone set. If it falls out, the process starts over again. Trial and error will quickly teach you how much glue is just enough. G-S Hypo-Tube Cement can be purchased at a craft or hobby store, a store that caters to rock hounds, and numerous places online. Fire Mountain Gems is online and offers a large catalog by calling 1-800-423-2319.

One repair you should not attempt is soldering. This is a job best left for professionals. Costume jewelry requires special handling before it can be soldered and some pieces may not even be possible to solder. And it is not inexpensive, so take that into consideration before purchasing a piece that will need soldering. I have heard there are some costume jewelry repair people who do a great job with soldering, but since I have not had it done, I am not recommending anyone.

Selling Your Jewelry

At some time you may decide to sell your jewelry. One of the best places to sell it is to other jewelry collectors. You can find many listed in the Maloney's Antiques & Collectibles Resource Directory. You can purchase it online at www.maloneysonline.com or from your local bookstore.

Many of the online jewelry clubs have a member's directory. Costume jewelry dealers are another good source, but you need to know right up front, they will only pay between 30% and 40% of the value of the jewelry. Consignment shops that have higher end clothing or vintage clothing are also good sources for selling vintage costume jewelry. Antiques publications such as AntiqueWeek have a classified ads section that may have jewelry buyers listed.

If you decide to sell your jewelry at an online auction, remember to keep it simple. Collectors want to see the jewelry right now, or they will move on to the next treasure. Do NOT use fancy backgrounds, or music, or little animated anythings; these take too much time to load and most buyers will NOT wait. They don't want to be entertained, they want to buy something.

Describe the jewelry in the best detail you can, noting any signatures or marks, give measurements and take photos of the back of the jewelry as well as the front. You don't have to be an expert, just be accurate. Look at other listings before doing your own. If the jewelry is signed, do a search for that name, and see what other people have to say about it. But remember, not everyone is truthful and some people are simply misinformed.

If you don't have a digital camera that can do close ups, put the jewelry right onto the scanner bed. It is ALWAYS worth the extra effort and cost to add the photo of the back of the jewelry to the description. To many collectors, the back of the jewelry is as important as the front.

Vintage Ads

The antique show had a booth selling ads and I made a beeline for it. My brother collects Volkswagen memorabilia, and they always have some good VW ads. I like to hang Coca-Cola ads in my kitchen and I am always looking for new ones. It never occurred to me to look for jewelry ads, until a friend recently told me someone had some for auction.

At first I thought this would be something great to hang in my office. Of course I love the jewelry, but I also loved the ladies who appeared in some of these ads. Ladies from my great-grandmother's generation, who never left the house without wearing a hat and gloves.

Then I spotted a Trifari ad from a 1959 issue of *Vogue* magazine. There was the Trifari pin and earrings I had in my own collection. I had always thought of this set as a type of cascade, but it is from a line called "Etoilé" which retailed for $7.50 to $35.50. How very exciting! It turns out these ads are not just of a decorative nature.

Isabel "Liz" Bryman (www.lizjewel.com) agrees. "I think of vintage ads as important historical artifacts. They have been ignored far too long as worthless, I believe. Ads document WHAT people liked, WHAT they bought, HOW they viewed and lived their lives through products and services they selected. Ads mirror CHANGES, transitions; in lifestyles, mindsets, tastes, innovations, even better than most other publications."

Bryman continues, "Today we don't see too many ads for trolley fare cards, buggy whips or travel by airship, agree? Instead we see ads for cell phones, cable television, and jet travel, which obviously were not available in the past. Ads are a continuous documentary of how our lives change because of new innovations." She collects ads, she states, "because I draw on them for dating antiques, collectibles and other reasons. If an ad can be established as published in a certain year, the product in it is also dated. And I use ads for my research."

And speaking of research, ads are invaluable in detecting fakes and reproductions, as they show the original designs for each piece.

The best ads for vintage costume jewelry date from the 1940s and 1950s. *Vogue*, *Harper's Bazaar*, and *Town & Country* are some of the magazines that have ads for the jewelry that most of us seek. Almost all the designers you can think of can be found, with some diligence. Haskell, Schiaparelli, Bogoff, Trifari, Eisenberg and Coro are most often found, and designers like Weiss, Rosenstein and Mazer less available. I have even found an ad showing the original colors of Bakelite, to add to my new collection of Bakelite. Most of the ads dealers I have seen at shows and malls do not carry many jewelry ads, and those that do usually have either fine jewelry or watches.

All of the ads in my personal collection have been obtained on the Internet, where there are dealers specializing in ads of all types. The hardest thing to find these days is a complete magazine, as the best ones are taken apart to sell the ads separately.

Ads can usually be found for around five dollars, with color ads and those with more popular designers and jewelry going for up to ten dollars. I did see an ad last summer that went for several hundred dollars, in a bidding war between two bidders. Apparently one had a beautiful piece of jewelry that was unmarked, and the ad gave a definitive maker to the piece, making the value of the jewelry much more than without the provenance of the ad. Much, MUCH more.

When you look for these ads, don't just look for the jewelry ads. Many movie stars posed with fine and costume jewelry, and some of the couture ads are fabulous. They are perfect compliments to each other in your collection.

Many websites offering vintage costume jewelry are also featuring ads the owners of the sites have collected. One of these is Jane Clarke, who has a booth in an antique mall and a wonderful, informative website. Clarke's Morning Glory Antiques and Jewelry (www.morninggloryantiques.com) is one of the best places to go when you have hours to read and peruse. Her site offers all the best in vintage costume jewelry, divided by designer, making it easy to shop for your favorites. Then there are sections of articles she has written on jewelry, and the ads for it, and a section featuring movie star ads. These can be found under the heading JewelChat.

Clarke says, "Old jewelry ads are wonderful references of both dates and designs of earlier jewelry makers, as well as how the jewelry was originally worn and by whom. In some cases, it is about the only way we have of tracking when pieces were made. So much of the very best was made during the 40/50s and many people who were personally involved are elderly or gone now. . . . it is so important that we document all we can. That's one of the reasons I started JewelChat (www.jewelchat.com). It is a place to collect and share all the pictures, ads, history and anecdotes possible about the jewelry we all love so much!"

Clarke has even gone one step further for De Rosa jewelry. She has obtained hand-painted illustrations from the De Rosa Jewelry Company, which are miniature pieces of artworks, and she showcases these alongside De Rosa ads and the actual jewelry.

Vintage ads are an affordable, informative and beautiful treasure. Add some to your collection today.

Harper's Bazaar, 1949.

Les Fleurs
delicately fashioned pins
and earrings... perfect gifts
at fine stores
everywhere. From the
jewelry collection of

Adele Simpson

Vogue, 1946.

GARDEN PARTY... Petals that look like moonstones, touched with the sparkle of faraway stars:
white, light blue or multi-color with silver-toned settings;
yellow with gold-toned setting.
Necklace, bracelet, earrings, pin: each $2.00 plus tax. At fine stores everywhere.

ALL DESIGNS COPYRIGHT 1958 D. LISNER & CO., 393 FIFTH AVENUE, NEW YORK

McCall's, 1946.

JEWELS *Miriam Haskell*

AT SAKS FIFTH AVENUE, NEW YORK AND SMART STORES THROUGHOUT THE COUNTRY—MIRIAM HASKELL, 392 FIFTH AVENUE, NEW YORK, N. Y.

You can buy this merchandise at stores listed (Vogue's Buying Guide) p. 198.   VOGUE incorporating Vanity Fa

Vogue, 1951.

Imperial Mexican Jade

the correct jewelry accent for

Marlboro Cigarette-slim fashions

Gems of exotic beauty, recently unearthed in Old Mexico and known there as
Mexican Jade, now have the spotlight on the jewelry stage. Choice specimens of
Mexican Jade fashioned by America's foremost designers, are offered by Imperial as
the most beautiful jewels you could possibly wear with greys, browns, greens and
blacks. The mountings are sterling silver, hand-wrought with the skill that only
Aztec Mexico has for this work. Priced from $5 to $50, plus tax.

Imperial Gem Syndicate

607 Fifth Ave., New York 20, New York
5 N. Wabash Ave., Chicago 2, Illinois
607 S. Hill, Los Angeles 14, California

Vogue, 1943.

blues in the night

Bogoff presents for this season of
festive evenings . . . a study in blues . . . a blue
as blue as the Mediterranean . . . and a blue
with all the fiery brilliance of a sapphire . . .
achieving a diamond-like elegance in third
dimension . . . so distinctively Bogoff.

jewels by BOGOFF

Necklace, about 30.00
Bracelet, about 15.00
Slim Jim Earrings, about 12.00
Button Earrings, about 8.00
Pin, about 10.00
Other Jewels by Bogoff 1.00 to 30.00
plus tax

at fine stores everywhere
JEWELS BY BOGOFF · creators of fine costume jewelry · 366 Fifth Ave., New York · Chicago · Los Angeles
Only the original bears the name BOGOFF stamped on the back

McCall's, 1952.

Old designs translated into new jewelry by

Nettie Rosenstein

Harper's Bazaar, 1946.

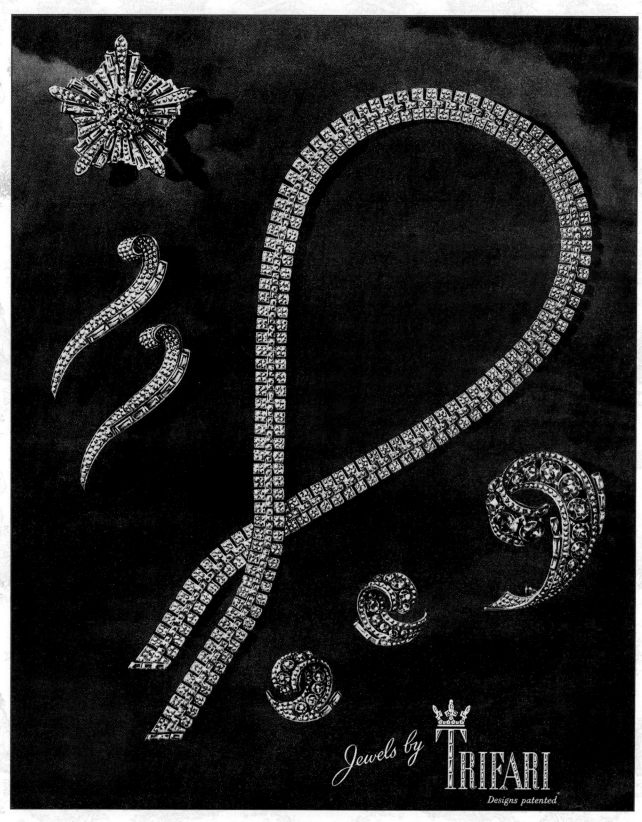

Vogue, 1946.

McCall's, 1945.

Harper's Bazaar, 1946.

CREATIONS TECLA

Ces deux bagues ravissantes sont montées sur platine avec de vrais diamants. Si la perle et l'émeraude étaient véritables, leur valeur s'élèverait à des centaines de mille francs. Cependant, leur perfection est telle que seul un examen minutieux par des experts peut les faire reconnaître.

Les perles Técla se font dans toutes les mêmes nuances et les mêmes grandeurs que les perles véritables.

Collier Técla 40 cm. fermoir or 250 Francs

Catalogue illustré sur demande

Técla

10 Rue de la Paix Paris
7. Old Bond Street Londres.
15, Unter den Linden Berlin W.
New York.

Modes Travaux, 1946.

DESIGNS COPYRIGHTED

Jewels of the elite® **CORAL RED FLOWERS** *fabulously carved and set in flashing crystal.* Necklace, 50.00; earrings, 20.00, plus tax.

Only at the finest stores

JOSEPH MAZER
29 West 36 St., New York 18, N. Y.

ALTER EGO . . . the shoe with a split personality . . . Red Shoe Red with black patent. About $9 at fine stores coast to coast. We'll tell you where. Cobblers, Inc., 1212 Stanford Ave., Los Angeles 21, Calif.

California **COBBLERS**

Vogue, 1958.

I couldn't find a thing

until...

"This case unscrambled my life. Now beads no longer tangle. (No more broken strands.) The biggest necklace fits neatly. The tiniest earring can't hide. Stones stay in their settings. Dust stays safely out. There's more than enough room for every piece I own. And I dress in ten seconds flat!"

Jewel Case by **LADY BUXTON**
best for your money

WHITE, BLACK, LIGHT BLUE, GOLD, $20.00—FROM A JEWEL CASE COLLECTION WITH A SIZE FOR EVERY NEED—$5.00 TO $42.50. PRICES SLIGHTLY HIGHER WEST OF THE ROCKIES. ©1962 BUXTON INC., SPRINGFIELD, MASS., BUXTON CANADA, LTD., TORONTO 9.

McCall's, 1960.

ESSO RESEARCH works wonders with oil

Oil you never see helps make beautiful jewelry

SIROCCO JEWELS BY COROCRAFT

*Creating the sparkling brilliance and perfect design in high-fashion jewelry . . .
that's the very last job you'd expect of oil! Yet Esso Research developed a special oil
to coat the metal, and help make the flawless shaping of these pieces possible.
Finding the right lubricant is one way* **ESSO RESEARCH** *works wonders with oil.*

Life, 1956.

Vogue, 1945.

Vogue, 1948.

A New Twist
in

*Eisenberg Ice**

Beautiful, blinding blaze of splendor
gem-set like the world's greatest jewels in
a new motif of rippling glitter. Pins, Earrings, Necklaces,
Bracelets, from $10.00 to $35.00 (plus tax).

EISENBERG JEWELRY, INC., 22 WEST MADISON ST., CHICAGO 2, ILL.

Vogue, 1953.

Costume Jewelry Internet Websites

There are now a tremendous amount of websites offering vintage costume jewelry. Some of the very best offer more than just jewelry for sale, many offer free educational tools. I have complied a list of my favorites sites, they are not in any type of order. No special ratings were used, these are merely my favorites. There are many other sites out there but most of these have stood the test of time. In addition to the ones listed, you can find many more vintage costume jewelry sites at larger "stores" such as Tias.com and RubyLane.com. These sites are both important, but their individual sites are too numerous to mention. They are easy to navigate when you are ready to shop their stores.

It was difficult to narrow the list for this book; there are some really wonderful websites, but it was not possible to feature every great site in this first book. Please take time to look at all the sites offering vintage costume jewelry; the web ring found at lizjewel.com will link you to over one hundred sites devoted to costume jewelry.

Each website was given the same questionnaire, which follows. Because of the economic times, some of these long term sites may have disappeared by the time the book has been published. I apologize for any confusion this may cause.

The Questionnaire:

Date your site started.
The owners' names.
What exactly do you carry?
What do you consider to be your specialty?
Is there any jewelry you are actively seeking?
Would you like sellers to contact you, and if so, how?
Does your site have a buyer's wish list?
Do you offer an email newsletter or update program?
Do you belong to any professional organizations?
Do you do appraisals?
Is there any additional information you would like included?

N&N Jewelry at Trifari.com
Neil and Natasha Cuddy (N&N)

N&N began as a website in January 1999, and since then has been continually updated, with what now totals thousands of items — you can see the update history here: http://trifari.com/new.html. In Internet years, we have been in business for decades: you can buy from us in confidence that you will receive what we photograph and describe.

We began dealing in jewelry twenty years ago, in England. We continued after our move to Canada in 1989. Since then, we have begun to specialize in the great costume jewelry of the classic period from the 1930s to the 1960s, when jewels were made from glass which were artistically more interesting and innovative than those including precious stones — and equally well made. They have of course remained so. If you take a tour of our site from the home page, through the designer and figural collections including Trifari, Boucher, Mazer, Chanel, Coro, Reja, Pennino, Dior, Eisenberg, Haskell, Carnegie, KJL, Ciner, Silson, Schiaparelli, you will see what we mean.

We chose our site domain (trifari.com) because we tend to specialize in jewels made by Trifari in their classic period (from the 1930s to the 1960s); a look at our five Trifari pages will make it clear that our Trifari collections are larger than those for other manufacturers. We have no connection with the modern Trifari company, which (along with the Monet group) was purchased as a brand in 2000 by the Liz Claiborne corporation.

We are always looking to buy high quality, interesting early designer pieces such as those featured on our Masterpiece collection: http://trifari.com/mpc.html

There is an email link to us on our site Trifari.com — or directly at sales@trifari.com

We don't offer a buyer's wish list — as it is often impossible to predict when we will have a particular piece in stock — many are rare and difficult to find and we may find a wanted piece tomorrow, in 5 years, or never. Yes — we update weekly, and inform over 1,000 customers with an email update. To be added, simply email us at sales@trifari.com, and say something along the lines of "add me to your email list"

N&N began dealing in jewelry twenty years ago, in England. Natasha has taken the FGA exam (Fellow of the Gemological Association of Great Britain) and Neil's academic history background (Oxford University PhD) accounts for the focus on patents and historical dating on our site.

Although we try to answer all email enquiring about identification and value — we expect Jewel Museum.com will fill this need. Trifari.com is often used for valuation purposes by many visitors — but we hope JewelMuseum.com will be much easier to use and very comprehensive.

Coming soon — JewelMuseum.com — a subscription site containing our archive of thousands of items, plus patents, catalogues, and all the dating and identification aids for vintage jewel collectors.

Eclectica at Eclecticala.com
Laurel Ladd Ciotti

Our first jewelry theme site has been on the web since May of 1997. Our main designer and collectible jewelry site, Eclectica, has been online since 1998.

We carry quality collectible vintage and designer jewelry from Victorian through the seventies. Plus, we now carry a small and select boutique line of current and contemporary designs on several of our specialty theme sites.

We sell a broad selection of quality vintage jewelry on our main site (www.eclecticala.com) but we are known on the web for our outstanding and large selections of cocktail rings, vintage charm bracelets (Just Charmed), as well as our terrific collections of vintage and contemporary ladybug jewelry at Just Ladybugs, and our unique selections of vintage guilloche enamels at Enamel Roses. (All theme sites may be accessed through our front page at www.eclecticala.com.)

We are always looking to buy great vintage jewelry! We actively look for colored rhinestones, sets, suites, and great styles, no matter the designer's name. We buy beautiful jewelry from all time periods, eras, and price ranges.

Sellers may email buyers@eclecticala.com or telephone 352-591-4630 from 10:00 AM to 6:00 PM Eastern time. Please have photographs available, a detailed description and your best price ready to discuss.

We keep a private list for all of our customers of their wants and wishes. All you need to do is email WTB@eclecticala.com and we will help you find your heart's desire (Want To Buy).

Eclectica has had a Preferred Customer List for several years. Preferred Customers learn of major updates before the general public and there are special offers and incentives available only through our Preferred Customer Mailings. To join, read about it on our Index page (www.eclecticala.com) or just email Preferred@eclecticala.com for details.

Member of Jewelcollect since 1997
Registered Member Club Jewelcollect since 1999.

While we are happy to share basic information and opinions online, we cannot give a truly accurate appraisal unless we can see and hold an item in person. Also, since we buy for resale, we try never to suggest a price for items we wish to buy since that is rather like asking the fox to guard the henhouse. We feel it unethical to name our own price when we wish to purchase an item.

Our jewelry sites include our large main site as well as at least 28 specialized and unique theme sites. We take pride in our reasonable prices and our excellent customer care and service.

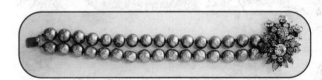

Morning Glory Antiques at morninggloryantiques.com
Jane Haley Clarke
Est. November 1995

Available: Vintage costume, designer, Bakelite, sterling and Victorian jewelry, purses, and accessories.

Specialize: DeRosa, Haskell, Trifari, Staret, Rosenstein, McClelland Barclay sterling, Victorian

Always seeking good-quality high-end or unusual pieces.

jane@morninggloryantiques.com.

Yes, both Jewel Chat online reference e-Zine and a buyer's update notification.

No appraisals.

Costume Jewelry Internet Websites

Plastic Fantastic at plasticfantastic.com
Karima Parry
Est. 1995
Available: High-end Bakelite, Shultz Bakelite, Lucite and fine jewelry

Specialize: Bakelite

info@plasticfantastic.com
Jewelcollect Registered Member, VFCJ

Author of three best-selling books on Bakelite jewelry; have written the *Plastically Yours* column for VFCJ for five years.

Barbara B. Wood's Vintage and Costume Jewelry at bwoodantiques.com

Barbara B. Wood's Vintage and Costume Jewelry site was started in 1997. I carry old Bakelite, and new Bakelite artists. I specialize in Shultz Bakelite and carry Judy Clarke's Lucite and Bakelite Art, Jackie Weeks Bakelite and Lucite Art, Karen Kronimus Bakelite, and Penny and Dan Lains Bakelite Jewelry. I also carry lots of signed designer costume jewelry, fine jewelry, purses, compacts, perfumes, and some of my favorite contemporary jewelry artists.

HoTx12@aol.com

I buy and sell and love vintage costume jewelry and some of my favorites are HAR, Schiaparelli, Schreiner, Trifari, Hollycraft, Florenza, Boucher, Ciner, Eisenberg, Hattie Carnegie, Hobé, Miriam Haskell, Swoboda, Edgar Berebi, Coppola e Toppo. I also love Matisse and Rebajes copper and old Mexican sterling. I carry both on my web site.

I am not a certified appraiser but do try to help people when I can. I also have a shop and another website on Yahoo's Shopping Website.

Liz Jewel at lizjewel.com
Isabelle "Liz" Bryman
Est. 1995

Available: A bit of everything in American and European vintage, silver, and with emphasis on American and European modern designer and runway jewelry; also introducing more and more ethnic/mystic jewelry (folk jewelry).

Specialize: I consider modern designer and runway jewelry to be my specialty, and am actively seeking them.

By email ibryman@lizjewel.com preferably, although I welcome phone calls also.

I used to do an email newsletter but found that announcements on Jewelcollect market days and on the JC Bulletin Board were more effective.
Jewelcollect and VFCJ (Vintage Fashion & Costume Jewelry Club).

No appraisals.

Jan's Jewels and More at jansjewels.com
Janice Kostura
Est. June 1996

Available: I carry a wide variety of costume jewelry, vintage jewelry-making supplies, and custom design jewelry. I also carry vintage patterns, sewing notions and vintage purses, vintage stones for jewelry repair.

Seeking: I collect Bird jewelry and some mosaics.

jan@jansjewels.com

I have a buyer's notification list that breaks down into jewelry, jewelry supplies and patterns. When buyers sign up they can list the items they are specifically looking for.

The International Jewelers Design Guild and Jewel Collect.

No appraisals, I leave that to the real experts.

I offer free jewelry-making instructions and have been adding at least two instructions each month. In March of 2003 I started a Monthly Design Challenge. I draw three names each month and send out supplies to the winners. They in turn send in a picture to share with my viewers. I have a stone conversions chart as well as some other resources information. Also available is a free Jewelry Assistant Program. This program covers beads, stones, wires, ring sizes, and a variety of other jewelry related info. For my sewing customers, there is a free vintage doll pattern available for download. I have something for just about everyone!

Emerald City Vintage Costume Jewelry at emcity.com
Elizabeth Rowlands
Est. June 1998

Available: Quality vintage costume jewelry emphasizing the "real-look" pieces of the 1930s – 1950s. Elegant pieces from Bogoff, Boucher, Trifari, Coro-Craft, Mazer, and more are my specialty and what I am actively seeking.

beth@emcity.com

No appraisals.

Resources and information are also available on the site. Occasional articles on designers, plus a standard feature with many vintage costume jewelry ads for reference.

Vintage Jewelry Arts and Antiques at vintagejewelryartsandantiques.com
Kim D. Paff
Est. March 12, 2002

Available: Vintage costume jewelry including but not limited to vintage Bakelite, new designer Bakelite, signed and unsigned designer costume jewelry; copper, enamel, and sterling silver jewelry; Victorian and fine jewelry, accessories including vintage purses, cigar box purses, hats and hair accessories, perfume bottles, household items, and collectibles.

Specialize: Vintage Bakelite

Seeking: Quality vintage costume jewelry and vintage accessories.

kim @vintagejewelryartsandantiques.com

I have a private notification list.

Registered member Jewelcollect, Vintage Fashion and Costume Jewelry Club, Jewelry Talk, Bakelite Jewels and Bakelite Collectors Club, Certified Appraiser, Certified Antique and China Conservation Restoration Artist.

I appraise certified jewelry and personal property (i.e., antiques appraiser).

AZillion SPARKLZ Vintage Costume Jewelry & Fine Estate Jewelry at sparklz.com
Janet W. Lawwill
Est. Feb. 1997

Available: Vintage costume jewelry including Victorian, Deco, Nouveau, rhinestone, designer, plastics, copper, Mexican silver, Southwestern silver, beads, figurals, patriotic, sweetheart, cufflinks, ivory, and Christmas; some contemporary designer costume jewelry, and fine vintage estate jewelry.

Specialize: Extremely broad variety of the website in number of jewelry items, all eras, all types of jewelry.

AZillion SPARKLZ is always buying better costume jewelry, designer costume jewelry, fine estate jewelry, and ivory jewelry.

jewel@sparklz.com. Information page for sellers: www.sparklz.com/buy/buy.htm.

Buyer's wish list and email update program.

Vintage Fashion Costume Jewelry, Glittering Times, National Cufflink Society, Jewelcollect Registered Members Club.

Evaluation Clinics.

Telephone number: 520-907-2839.
Address: AZillion SPARKLZ/Janet Lawwill
      P. O. Box 36269
      Tucson, AZ 85740-6269
Website URL: www.sparklz.co

Helpful information on the website: Costume Jewelry

Costume Jewelry Internet Websites

Cleaning, Repair Guide & Resources; Building a Rhinestone Inventory; Identification of Materials: About Cameos, About Ivories, About Amber, About Enamels.

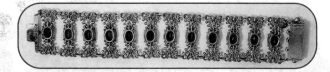

Bijoutree's Jeweled Forest at christmastreepins.com
Kathy Flood
Est. August 2000

Available and Specialize: Christmas tree pins. Also carry general vintage costume jewelry with an emphasis on figurals. Tracking down hard-to-find holiday brooches . . . all year long!

Seeking: Christmas tree pins and interesting figurals. For my own collection I am looking especially for the Marie Ferra, NBC, and HAR Christmas tree pins.

bizstyle@aol.com or Admin@christmastreepins.com

The Jeweled Forest offers a combination newsletter and update via email.

VFCJ and Jewelcollect.

No appraisals.

As a collector, I take pleasure in getting to know fellow collectors and sharing in the excitement of finding costume jewelry we all love. I'm happy to look for special pieces and willing to offer an informed opinion on jewelry, especially Christmas tree pins, when collectors are curious or concerned.

Illusion Jewels at illusionjewels.com
George and Dotty Stringfield
Est. April 1997

Available: Vintage costume jewelry, contemporary jewelry by Dorothea.

Specialize: Offering lovely vintage jewelry at reasonable prices.
jewels@illusionjewels.com

Email update program offered.

VFCJ, Jewelcollect, International Jewelry Designers Guild (IJFG).

No appraisals.

Researching Costume Jewelry, at illusionjewels.com/list.html, is an extensive list of costume jewelry designers and companies with dates and historical information. Much of the information is from research Pat Seal of Joshua, TX, has done in periodical libraries. This resource is continuing to grow and change as new information is found.

Rhinestone Rainbow at rhinestonerainbow.com
Deborah Kosnett
Est. 1997

Available: Vintage costume jewelry, specializing in the decades of the 30s, 40s, 50s, and 60s. I also specialize in enamels, flowers, figurals, and the wacky and offbeat.

Buyers are welcome to e-mail me with a listing of things they are looking for, and I will let them know if I run across it.

I send out emails when I update the site.

Vintage Fashion and Costume Jewelry club.

No appraisals.

My site offers educational information regarding so-called fake vintage jewelry, as well as links to other educational pages.

B'sue Boutiques at bsueboutiques.com
Brenda Sue Lansdowne
Est. 1997

Ours is a very special site because we not only carry

over 500 well-priced pieces of vintage jewelry from costume to designer names, but we also carry contemporary artisan works as well as play to those who need to make repairs on old jewelry. We nurture the artisan spirit. We have an extensive selection of repair stones, designer stones, rare old vintage components and Victorian-style brass stampings in many finishes, as well as beading supplies and all the tools you need to do basic repairs.

We are always buying, but I would say I would be more interested in well-priced early twentieth century pieces, especially old Czech, West German, pot metal figurals, and designer names.

bsue1441@aol.com

To be added to our email list, just send me an email.

Check our Ebay store; there are 500 items loaded there constantly: http://www.stores.ebay.com/bsueboutiques-jewelrysupplies.

Yes, I am a charter member of VFCJ and write two columns for every issue. I also am an active member of Jewelcollect since 1997.

Appraisals for an hourly fee.

Aurora Bijoux Costume Jewelry at aurorabijoux.com
Jenny Stephens
Est. July 1997

Available: Costume jewelry with an emphasis on vintage and retro pieces. Additional inventory includes vintage smalls and contemporary costume jewelry suitable for bridal, prom, and special events.

Specialize: Vintage costume jewelry.

Seeking: LN L/N LN/25; important glitz by Alice Caviness.

aurora@aurorabijoux.com or via phone: 215-872-7808.

Email update program.

VFCJ, JC, NMOA (National Mail Order Association).

Market value appraisals.

Owner of Bubbles-n-Baubles.com — a one stop shop for all jewelry cleaning needs, and JewelryJoose.com — manufacturer of products specifically for cleaning vintage and antique costume and fine jewelry.

Designer Costume Jewelry at valerieg.com
Valerie B. Gedziun
Est. July 1997

Available: Vintage and contemporary American and European jewelry, fashion watches.

Specialize: Vintage couture jewelry by Chanel, Gripoix, Givency, Galalith (French Bakelite), contemporary one-of-a-kind jewelry. I travel to France and Europe every year to search for new merchandise.

Seeking: French designer jewelry.

valg@attbi.com

Vintage Fashion & Costume Jewelry member, Jewelcollect Registered Member Club.

No appraisals.

We feature the jewelry of Histoire de Verre, the contemporary line of the House of Gripoix. Each piece is hand made using the poured glass methods developed by Madame Gripoix in the 30s.

Black Cat Collectibles at blackcatcollectibles.com
Wendy Hankins
Est. March 1997

Available: Vintage costume jewelry from approximately 1910 – 1970. Emphasis is on the 40s & 50s rhinestone pieces. I have quite a large selection of signed pieces, but also carry lots of unsigned. I have a small amount of Bakelite and other plastics, some silver and copper, and quite a few strands of beads. I try to keep my prices affordable. I carry mostly lower-priced and mid-priced items. Lots of stuff in the $25 – $35 range

Specialize: Mid-priced unsigned rhinestones from the 40s and 50s.

Seeking: Juliana, fruit salad pieces, unsigned Haskell. But, it has to be cheap.

No appraisals.

Whiskey Creek Jewels at whiskey-creek.net
Lorie and Mark Mattson
Est. 1997

Available: Vintage signed and unsigned costume jewelry to include several pages of Christmas items, figurals, and florals, silver and copper pieces, cameos, usually Edwardian-Victorian pieces, and shortly I will showcase my own designs.

Specialize: Vintage designer jewelry and Edwardian-Victorian jewelry.

Seeking: Early Coro pieces, Castlecliff jelly belly 1" animals, and tremblers, early enamels, cameos (including Juliana cameos).

Whiskey Creek Jewels
P.O. Box 2956
Stockbridge Georgia 30281
info@whiskey-creek.net

Update system.

No appraisals.

I do costume jewelry repair and am available for seminars.

Carole Tanenbaum Vintage Collection at truefaux.com
Carole Tanenbaum.
Est. 1999

Available: We carry vintage costume jewelry including purses, compacts, hair accessories, buttons, and glass perfume bottles.

Specialize: We consider our specialty to be 1940s to 1950s costume jewelry including such designers as Schiaparelli, Schreiner, Eisenberg, Trifari, Hobé, Miriam Haskell. We are actively seeking — Sandor, complete sets, rare Bakelite items.

caroletanenbaum@sympatico.ca or carole258@sympatico.ca. Phone: 416-782-3005 Fax: 416-782-3720

Buyer's Wish list.

Update program twice a month.

Jewelcollect & the Professional Art Dealer Association.

Appraisals.

Our collection is based on what is currently trending in the fashion world. The collection and wish list changes from season to season based on what's popular. We always appreciate seller contact and feedback.

Just Jewelry at jstjewelry.com
Kim and Larry Cummins
Est. April 1, 1997

Available: We carry quality vintage costume jewelry, most of it from the 1940s – 1960s.

Specialize: We specialize in signed or designer pieces. Larry does most of the buying, and he has always felt that buying signed pieces was a better investment.

Seeking: We actively seek high-end Schiaparelli. We also look for Sandor, especially the older enamel-over-sterling pieces. Other designers I look for are Napier (those pieces made before the 1970s), HAR figurals or other unusual HAR pieces, and KJL dragons. I have been searching for a 1960s Trifari serpent necklace with blue glass drops for what seems like forever. Whenever possible, I try to buy quality signed necklace and earring sets or whole parures.

Sellers can contact us by phone: 618-398-2173, or by email: kdcllc@peaknet.net.

I have an email list/newsletter I send out when I update my site. Those interested can email me to be put on the list.

I have belonged to Vintage Fashion and Costume Jewelry Newsletter Club and Jewelcollect Listserv since 1997.

No appraisals.

In Memoriam 03-18-1969 – 03-12-2004
Katie Atikian Antiques at kateroo.com
Katie Atikian
Est. October 2000.

Available: Vintage Jewelry of all types — including a wide assortment of costume jewelry by various designers, such as Boucher, Hattie Carnegie, Coro, Kramer, Eisenberg, Miriam Haskell, Hobé, Hollycraft, Joseff of Hollywood, Alexander Korda, Mazer/Jomaz, Mimi di N., Regency, Original by Robert, and Weiss. Danish & Norwegian sterling, Mexican sterling, and Danecraft sterling jewelry. A very large selection of copper jewelry by Matisse, Renoir & Rebajes.

Speciality: Really, jewelry of all types, but I have a huge selection of copper by Matisse, Renoir & Rebajes, and am an expert on Matisse/Renoir, and have done extensive research on the company as well as written an article.

Appraisers National Association; American Bar Association; California Bar Association (I am a licensed California attorney as well).

Copper jewelry specialist.

Eureka, I Found It! Antiques and Collectibles at eureka-I-found-it.com
Susan
Est. 1997

Available: We feature a variety of vintage costume jewelry, both signed and unsigned, and sterling silver jewelry.

Specialty: Figurals and offbeat designs.

I maintain a Wanted to Buy list for specific items.

If requested, I will notify buyers of updates.

No appraisals.

I buy what I like, which is unusual designs that make a statement. No conservative jewelry here! I am very fussy about condition and choose to buy only those pieces in excellent condition, with no noticeable flaws. I also offer a satisfaction guaranteed policy. Items may be returned for any reason.

Sue's Jewels at spilot.com
Sue Sinclair
Est. 1999

Available: Vintage Costume Jewelry

Specialize: Copper, Bakelite (vintage and jewelry that my husband and I make from old raw stock) and other plastics, colorful rhinestones, medium-priced designer pieces.

Seeking: Mostly 1940s and 1950s signed pieces, but I hunt for a wider selection for my customers. We carry silver and Native American jewelry too.

spilot@atlantic.net

Jewelcollect, VFCJ.

No appraisals.

There is a show schedule on my website where the jewelry can be seen.

Costume Jewelry Internet Websites

South Texas Trading Company at
southtexastrading.com
BeeGee McBride
Est. 1997

Available: Vintage, costume, and designer jewelry, and Original Christmas Tree Pins by BeeGee

Specialize: Unusual vintage pieces, especially figurals.

Seeking: I am always seeking plastic (Bakelite, Lucite, and celluloid) figural pieces, and any costume pieces for resale.

STFNandTrading@centurytel.net

Keep a wish list electronically.

Mailing list.

Appraisals.

VFCJ, Jewelcollect, International Jewelry Design, Jewelry Talk.

I am always interested to hear from Alexander KORDA collectors.

Bakelite Boutique at bakeliteboutique.com
Ava Solomon Polan
Est. January 2001

Available: Vintage Bakelite and celluloid jewelry and Bakelite and Lucite purses.

Specialize: High-end Bakelite bangles.

Seeking: High-end vintage Bakelite jewelry and purses.

ava@bakeliteboutique.com

Appraisals.

My website showcases some of the finest vintage Bakelite jewelry available for sale anywhere!

Garden Party Collection at costumejewel.com
Adrienne Shivers
Est. October 1997

Available: All types of vintage costume jewelry, ranging from Victorian up through about the 60s, with a few contemporary pieces thrown in.

My specialty is selection. I have everything from $15.00 fun-but-not-important items to high-end important vintage costume pieces worth hundreds. The site currently has close to 1,000 items in inventory, so there's something for everyone. My best customers are the collectors and lovers of jewelry for all occasions.

I'm always buying, but currently I am actively hunting bracelets, necklaces, and parures of big, flashy, colorful rhinestones, Deco and Czech pieces, Schreiner, and Schiaparelli.

info@costumejewel.com

Wish list.

Email update program.

I've been told my site is extremely easy to navigate, despite its size. It's e-commerce enabled, making shopping a breeze. And I work hard to make the online buying experience easy and pleasurable, including an unconditional guarantee policy. There's also a consignment section active on the site, for those wishing to sell online but without the means. Details are available on the site.

Antique and Costume Jewelry Replacement Stones at
mrstones.com and sparklz.com/matt
Matthew Ribarich

Available: Over 6 million vintage and costume jewelry replacement stones.

Specialize: Having about 90 different colors of Rhinestones and shapes or sizes that have not been made in years. Also in stock is a great selection of Marcasites in rounds, squares, and baguettes.

My phone number is also a fax number: 757-558-9997. E-mail at MRstones4U@aol.com.

A current catalog is sent with every order.

VFCJ and Jewelcollect.

No appraisals.

We do everything from single stone replacement to complete restoring of jewelry, like Eisenberg, Trifari, Coro Duettes, and Mazer.

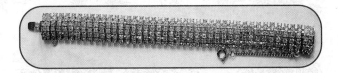

ChicAntiques at ChicAntiques.com
Pamela Wiggins
Est. 1995, started as Depression Delights

Available: A variety of moderately priced designer and quality unsigned vintage costume jewelry as well as Bakelite and other plastics. Also carry vintage ladies' accessories such as compacts, solid perfumes, hats, and handbags.

Specialize: Designer jewelry from the 1950s.

Seeking: 1950s Napier pieces, rhinestone jewelry with foiled and art glass stones, all quality signed and unsigned vintage pieces priced for resale.

Snail mail at PO Box 745, Round Rock TX 78680 or pam@chicantiques.com.

I accept wish lists by email.

Upon request I will email individuals when the site has been updated.

VFCJ, Austin Vintage Jewelry Club (serve as club coordinator).

Written appraisals are done on a limited basis for a fee based on the amount of research required. Verbal estimations of value are done as well, also for a fee.

I also sell jewelry at the Austin Antique Mall in Austin, Texas, and serve as the Antiques Guide for About.com (www.antiques.about.com).

The Family Jools at familyjools.com
Sheryl Hamilton
Est. 1998

Available: Vintage costume & fine jewelry, vintage purses and accessories, contemporary and artist jewelry. I like to think of my site as an "online boutique" as I ONLY sell on the Internet.

Specialize: (1) Vintage rhinestone jewelry, especially Canadian-made Sherman jewelry (2) my own SGH Original Designs and (3) the only known Sherman information pages on the Internet at http://www.familyjools.com/Sherman/ShermInfo/sherminfo.html.

Seeking: Sherman rhinestone jewelry, Art Deco jewelry, and purses.

sgh@familyjools.com . . . by phone at 403-239-0792 . . . or by fax at 403-239-9802. Items must be priced and in very good to excellent condition; I don't make offers.

Email updates and a Sherman collectors email list.

VFCJ and Jewelcollect, Joolcrafting (discussion group for jewelry artists) . . . and IJDG, the International Jewelry Designers' Guild (an online association of jewelry artists).

No appraisals.

My website was featured a couple of years ago in *InStyle* magazine! A very proud moment in The Family Jools history!

Fabulous Facets at cooljools.com
Lynda Hartwell
Est. 1998

Available: Vintage and antique costume and fine jewelry from 1840 – 1980.

Specialty: All of it!

oblyn@sover.net

Email newsletter.

Costume Jewelry Internet Websites

No appraisals.

My web site offers comprehensive information for the jewelry collector, including the following topics: Jewelry Bookstore, Gem History, Birthstones, Jewelry Designers Hall of Fame, Evolution of Coro Trademarks; Micro mosaic jewelry: What it is, and what it isn't; Misleading Gem Names, 18th & 19th Century Photo Gallery: Our Ancestors & Their Jewels.

Jazzle Dazzle at jazbot.com/Jazz
Lisa Botsko
Est. December 1999

Available: Vintage jewelry, including Victorian, Edwardian, Art Deco, Czech, French/Italian/Japan/German glass jewelry, Lucite/Bakelite and other plastics, designer-signed costume jewelry, unsigned costume jewelry, copper/wood/other ethnic theme jewelry, vintage sunglasses, purses, and hats.

Specialty: Vintage jewelry, particularly Czech. Goofus glass pins, Swoboda, Lea Stein, Denning copper enamel jewelry, California Pottery (Elzac) Victims of Fashion brooches.

Seeking: The type of jewelry featured on my website — Czech in particular. I am also actively seeking painted wood (or other material) bracelets with interesting themes/scenes.

Sellers are free to email via the email link on my website. Sellers must provide JPEG images of items for sale, thorough description of condition and defects, as well as asking prices of items available. I do not under any circumstances make offers.

Email website update for those who request to be on the mailing list.

Jewelcollect, Vintage Fashion and Costume Jewelry (VFCJ).

No appraisals.

Jazzle Dazzle has a structured discount program based upon larger purchases of multiple items.

Vintage Treasures at vintagejewelry.com
Brenda Nurenberg
Est. 1997

Specialize in upscale vintage costume jewelry that is in exceptionally good condition and offer a no-questions-asked return policy. I have a large selection of both signed and unsigned vintage costume jewelry pins, necklaces, earrings, and bracelets. I have some of the most sought after collector pieces of jewelry available online. I also have a large selection of vintage Christmas tree pins and Czechoslovakian necklaces.

Seeking older Trifari, Coro, Pennino, Schiaparelli, Mazer, and KJL in excellent condition. I also would love to find more jelly bellies.

I am always buying jewelry that is in excellent condition, and I can be emailed at luvglitz@AOL.com.

If buyers have a wish list, they can email me and I will keep that information on file.

Customers have the option to join my email list in order to receive updates of new jewelry recently added to the site. It is easy to join and just as easy to be removed from the list just by a request.

Vintage Fashion and Costume Jewelry Club, Jewelcollect.

No appraisals.

Deja-Voodoo at deja-voodoo.com
Ellen and Ned Solway
Est. August 2001

Available: High-end designer vintage costume to fun, flashy costume jewelry, quality figurals, and fantasy animal pins, chunky carved Bakelite bracelets and figural pins, as well as silver from Native American and Mexican to European and American studios. Mod.

Specialize: Schreiner of New York, Trifari, and Czech in costume; in silver American and European mod.

Seeking: High-end large costume pieces, figurals, Bakelite and American studio silver.

elned@cruzio.com
Jewelcollect.

No appraisals.

We've been in the vintage jewelry business for 16 years, and are on a constant hunt for unusual and interesting items. We are very picky about condition, and try to only show jewels that are in excellent shape. Once in a while something comes along that is too good to pass up and we will point out anything you should know in the listing.

**Annis Original Art Jewelry at
annisoriginalartjewelry.com**
Annie Navetta
Est. May, 2002

Available: Original jewelry designs, most of which are made with vintage glass beads and components (new old stock — I do not take apart old jewelry). I also sell vintage costume jewelry.

Specialty: Hand-wired floral collage necklaces and bracelets.

Anni@Annisoriginalartjewelry.com

E-mail update program.

The International Jewelry Designers' Guild

No appraisals.

I'm happy to work with buyers on adjustments (simple adjustments are free) and on custom orders.

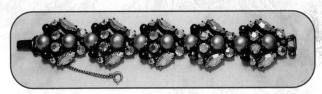

Cristobal at cristobal.co.uk
Steven Miners and Yai
Est. 1997

Available: All makes of high-quality costume jewelry from 1870 to the present day; you name it we have it, we specialize in Trifari, Miriam Haskell, Christian Dior, Joseff of Hollywood, Schreiner, Weiss, Coro Duette, Schiaparelli, Boucher, Mazer, Jomaz, etc.

MOOMOOLAND@aol.com

Buyer's wish list.

No appraisals.

Vintage Fashion & Costume Jewelry

This information is from the VFCJ brochure, and is used with permission:

Vintage Fashion and Costume Jewelry Club (VFCJ) was begun in late 1990 with an idea that there had to be one place where the history of the costume jewelry business could be recorded accurately. The idea of a newsletter was born, and since that time, the first 4-page black and white issue has grown into a 28-page slick, color-filled magazine. As the newsletter developed, the idea of a club became a reality. The Club sponsored its first national/international convention in 1993, drawing members from as far away as Japan and Germany in addition to bringing the people of the industry together with our membership. In 2003, we hosted our sixth national convention in Rhode Island. We meet there to acknowledge Rhode Island's place in the history of costume jewelry. During the off years, since our members so enjoyed their conventions, individuals have taken the initiative and have sponsored mini conventions. We have enjoyed meeting in the following sites: Lu Verne, Iowa; Los Angeles, California; Atlanta, Georgia; Chicago, Illinois; Seattle, Washington; Appleton, Wisconsin; Austin and Dallas, Texas; Sparta, New Jersey, and various places in Massachusetts. Most members attending have met just once, but some have developed into ongoing clubs. In addition, we have been able to work in close collaboration with the Providence Jewelry Museum to bring to bring our two associations together since our goals are so closely attuned. We welcome new members. If anyone wishes to join, please contact me at the address below.

Lucille Tempesta
P.O. Box 265
Glen Oaks, NY 11004
VFCJ@aol.com

Jewelcollect

I have been a member of Jewelcollect off and on since 1997. I highly recommend that all costume jewelry collectors join, at least briefly, for the opportunity to meet other collectors and see what is going on in the vintage costume jewelry world. Many of the foremost collectors and dealers of vintage costume jewelry subscribe to Jewelcollect. One feature of Jewelcollect is the Designer of the Week, which showcases the jewelry of a particular designer and gives members a chance to share photos of that designer's work from their own collections. Another feature has been the charity auctions that have raised thousands of dollars for charities such as the American Cancer Society and the Susan G. Komen Foundation. There is another level of membership, called Registered Jewelcollect Members, who agree to high standards of doing business. For more information, go to lizjewel.com and click on Jewelcollect.

About Jewelcollect (an interview with Isabelle "Liz" Bryman) :

Want to join the foremost email list serve for Collectible Jewelry, Jewelcollect? It's free to subscribers and has, since November 1995, managed to become the country club for networking, buying, selling, and exchanging information in this important niche. Commercial endeavors and enterprises are encouraged on Jewelcollect.

Many JC subscribers have met in person after meeting on Jewelcollect, done business together, and generally networked to mutual benefit. Some web page owners have added "Member Jewelcollect" to their list of credits. Most JC subscribers with web pages have them all linked to each other, in one large Collectible Costume Jewelry megamall. They also feel that to be a recognized and respected contributor/subscriber gives them instant and valuable credibility on the Internet.

It is my hope and goal that all members of Jewelcollect will find common interests and new friends through the list, and that we all will be able to exchange jewelry, monies, and confidences in complete trust among us. Anyone who violates this trust and does not live up to their promises is no longer welcome on Jewelcollect. We may have our differences of opinion but will always try to seek an amicable solution to any misunderstandings, with better communication being paramount.

As a subscriber to Jewelcollect, you meet 100% of your collectible niche — where can you top that? You get the pulse on what collectors like and seek, what dealers need, what the concerns, ethics, and fashions are, what is live and dead in collecting, buying, and selling jewelry, and meet a large group of very diversified professional people who have at least these things in common, but often more: love for vintage fine costume jewelry and great enthusiasm for the technical possibilities to further their hobbies or businesses.

The January/February 1997 issue of *Jewelry Crafts Magazine* featured a 4-page article highlighting Jewelcollect and its members, with a list of some of their web pages. Karey Miller Navo, publisher/owner, wrote the article, and she is, of course, a subscriber/member of Jewelcollect. The major costume jewelry club in the U.S., Vintage Fashion & Costume Jewelry Club, its newsletter, and it's owner, Lucille Tempesta, are among the regular members, as are several authors of costume jewelry reference and value guides and newsletters.

The following noted authors of costume jewelry reference works are present or recent past members of Jewelcollect: Harrice Simons Miller (*The Confident Collector, Faking It* [Kenneth Jay Lane biography]), Cherri Simonds (*Collectible Costume Jewelry*), Monica Lynn Clements and Patricia Rosser Clements (*Cameos: Classical to Costume*), Christie Romero (*Warman's Jewelry*), Matthew Burkholz (*The Bakelite Collection*), Sherry Shatz (*What Is It Made Of?*), Mary Morrison (*The Christmas Jewelry Book, The Snowbaby Book*), and Ginger Moro (*European Designer Jewelry*). Publishers of Costume Jewelry newsletters: Lucille Tempesta, Owner (*Vintage Fashion & Costume Jewelry Club*), and Davida Baron, Owner (*Glittering Times*). Designer Tomas Elefsiades designed the Jewelcollect club pin, Wendy Gell recently joined, and Brenda Sue Lansdowne, of B'Sue Boutiques jewelry line, is a longtime member. Other designers not currently online are networking with several members of Jewelcollect, notably Kenneth Lane, Larry Vrba, and David Mandel. Several jewelry manufacturers and/or dealers in Rhode Island, New York, Chicago, Dallas, Los Angeles, and other cities are also members. For more Jewelcollect members, visit the approximately 140 links to their web sites at: http://jewelcollect.org/. Click on Members Websites.

Jewelcollect

To further the hobby by exchanging information, and to reach out, express one's honest and humble opinion, share one's expertise and advice in a friendly, giving environment is what Jewelcollect is all about. Currently Jewelcollect has approximately 500 subscribers. Many come on board, stay a while and move on, but there is a core of very dedicated jewelry lovers who have helped build Jewelcollect from the beginning, and most of them are still subscribers.

If you wish to join, go to the pre-addressed email subscription form at: http://jewelcollect.org, Jewelcollect Organization, and click "Email Discussion List."

Follow directions on how to join. Your request will be forwarded to the owner for approval. When you receive the Welcome to Jewelcollect letter, you are on board. Posts (letters) will arrive to your email box, and you are invited to read and to participate by responding to the posts and by writing your own posts. The Welcome letter will have information (How to Participate) and posting guidelines and tips.

Isabelle Bryman (Liz)
ibryman@lizjewel.com
Owner-Administrator
Jewelcollect Listserv Email Club,
Exclusively Dedicated to Collectible
Costume Jewelry

Directory of Jewelcollect members who assisted with book.

Alice Leonard	Bobye Syverson
Davida Baron	Susan Hagadorn
Marsha Harrison	Diana Schommer
Judi Scheele	Janet Lawwill
Deb Schneider	Karima Parry
Harrice Simons Miller	Brenda Sue Lansdowne
Carol Johnston	Patricia Youngblood
Deborah Kosnett	Molly Garza
Pat Seal	Isabelle "Liz" Bryman
Jane Clarke	Kim Paff
Jenny Stephens	Elizabeth Nyland
Pam Cobb	Deborah Parker
Laurel Ladd Ciotti	Pamela Wiggins
Cheryl Killmer	Lori Mattson
Ginger Moro	Dotty Stringfield
Cathy Gordon	Joan Vogel Elias

Bibliography

Books

Baker, Lillian. *Fifty Years of Collectible Fashion Jewelry*. Paducah, KY: Collector Books, 1986.

Ball, Joanne Dubbs and Dorothy Hehl Torem. *Costume Jewelers, The Golden Age of Design*. Atglen, PA: Schiffer Publishing, 1990.

———· *Masterpieces of Costume Jewelry*. Atglen, PA: Schiffer Publishing, 1996.

Cera, Deanna Farneti. *Amazing Gems*. New York, NY: Harry Abrams Inc., 1995.

Dolan, Maryanne. *Collecting Rhinestone and Colored Jewelry*, 4th edition. Iola, WI: Books Americana, 1998.

Gordon, Angie. *Twentieth Century Costume Jewelry*. New York, NY: Adasia International, 1990.

Miller, Harrice Simons. *Costume Jewelry Identification and Price Guide*, 2nd edition. New York, NY: Avon Books, 1994.

Moro, Ginger H. *European Designer Jewelry*. Atglen, PA: Schiffer Publishing, 1995.

Parry, Karima. *Bakelite Bangles Price & Identification Guide*. Iola, WI: Krause Publications, 1999.

———· *Bakelite Pins*. Atglen, PA: Schiffer Publishing, 2001.

Pullée, Caroline. *20th Century Jewelry*. Emmaus, PA: JG Press, 1997.

Rezazadeh, Fred. *Costume Jewelry, A Practical Handbook & Value Guide*. Paducah, KY: Collector Books, 1998.

Simonds, Cherri. *Collectible Costume Jewelry Identification & Values*. Paducah, KY: Collector Books, 1997.

Di Noto, Andrea, ed. *The Encyclopedia of Collectibles, Inkwells to Lace*. Alexandria, VA: Time-Life Books, 1997.

Tolkien, Tracy and Henrietta Wilkinson. *A Collector's Guide to Costume Jewelry*. Ontario, Canada: Firefly Books, 1997.

Auction Catalog

Miller, Harrice Simons. *Christie's East Couture Jewels: The Designs of Robert Gossens*. New York, NY: Christie's Auction House, September 2000.

Index